THE SEVENTEEN PROVINCES

UNDER SPANISH RULE   (LATER TO BECOME HOLLAND AND BELGIUM)

This map shows the area, in which the story of *The Broken Chalice* unfolds, as it might have been around 1540. Through centuries of land reclamation activities and occasional losses to the sea the contour of the land has changed considerably since then. The area became known as the Netherlands after 1648. Later, in the year 1830, the predominantly Catholic southern provinces seceded to become present-day Belgium. The probable road between Flanders and Friesland taken by the van den Houtes is marked, and many places where a strong Anabaptist-Mennonite witness existed — even if no organized congregations were possible — are indicated on this map.

NORTH GOSHEN
MENNONITE CHURCH

NORTH SEA

Discard

Discard

Menno Simons was born at Witmarsum, Friesland. He served as a village priest at Pingjum for several years before joining the growing Anabaptist movement.

Menno Simons
and the church at Pingjum

THE
BROKEN
CHALICE

By Myron S. Augsburger

Illustrated by Edwin B. Wallace

HERALD PRESS, SCOTTDALE, PENNSYLVANIA

The Broken Chalice

"No human being was able to take away out of their hearts what they had experienced, such zealous lovers of God were they. The fire of God burned within them. They would die ten deaths rather than forsake the divine truth which they espoused." Such are the words a contemporary used to describe the Anabaptists.

Through the eyes of a wife and mother, *The Broken Chalice* gives insight into a family involved with the Anabaptist movement in Friesland. The reader will observe the two worlds as they collide.

Soetgen and Willem try to understand the movement and their friends involved in it. It is not until an itinerant preacher called Menno Simons comes to their home that they start to understand commitment to the true church.

This is a story about real people who lived and died. An account of their lives will be found on pages 646 to 651 in *Martyrs Mirror*. As Soetgen expressed in her last letter to her children before her death: "Take an example from the prophets and apostles; yea, Christ Himself, who all went this way; and where the head has gone before, there the members must surely follow."

Preface

The Free Church was the third wing of the Reformation and the background of Mennonite, Baptist, and related groups. In this book I have sought to re-express their faith for today's reader. Having expressed something of the movement in a previous novel, *Pilgrim Aflame*, this second one is written to represent women of the movement. Students of church history have pointed out that the attitude toward women in the Reformation was medieval in both the Catholic and Protestant groups, except among the Anabaptists or Free Church wing.

Fritz Blanke in his book, *Brothers in Christ*, in a footnote on page 77 writes: "That women were gripped by the revival in such a personal way that they stand up and request baptism is unusual for the Reformation period, and shows that within the Anabaptist movement women gained religious independence."

This novel is fictionalized history. The leading characters are actual persons and the major events actually happened according to information gleaned from the contents of letters to friends, family, or church group.

The letters from which much of the historical background has been found are as follows found in the *Martyrs Mirror*:

"A Testament of Soetgen van den Houte, . . ." pages 646-650

"A Letter of Soetgen van den Houte to Her Brother and Sister, as also to Her Children," pages 650-1.

A Confession of Faith of Jacques d'Auchy, . . ." pages 591-610

"Confession of a Woman Called Claesken, . . ." pages 611-616.

"How Jacques d'Auchy Was Betrayed, . . ." which tells of the end of Mr. de Wael who betrayed him to the authorities, pages 610-11.

Another source of historical information was *The Complete Writings of Menno Simons* with selections taken from pages 92, 93, 96, 108-111, 117, 120-122.

The husband of the heroine of this novel has been given the Dutch name of Willem. His actual name according to *The Mennonite Encyclopedia*, Vol. IV, p. 570, was Ghislain de Meulenaere. The English translation of the *Martyrs Mirror* used the German names for the characters when it was translated from Dutch into German. This accounts for the differences between the spelling of the names of some of the characters in this book and that in the English *Martyrs Mirror*. For example, Heinrich becomes Hendrik; Betgen becomes Betken.

Special acknowledgment is due Jan Gleysteen, formerly of The Netherlands, now an artist at the Mennonite Publishing House and Mennonite historian, for his reading the manuscript and making suggestions in keeping with the life and culture of the people of Flanders and Friesland in The Netherlands.

Myron S. Augsburger, President
Eastern Mennonite College

1

With eyes upturned Soetgen van den Houte stood gazing into the evening sky. The soft blond hair around her face was gathered into a bun resting on her neck. Her stiff white cap had fallen back on her shoulders, hanging from a broad ribbon across her throat. A smile played across her face as she watched the gulls circle above her, while the arms of the windmill turned lazily in the breeze. A ladened basket sat by her feet while she paused for a moment to rest. The crying sounds of the gulls came to her, mingled with the sighing of the wind in the willows.

There was something noble and proud about this woman, standing quietly yet radiating zest for life. Her face was winsome, with slender nose and generous mouth. Her clear skin was brightened by a tinge of pink in the cheeks. Her eyes were large and bright, long lashes sweeping up toward finely arched brows. An open expression seemed to communicate a gracious spirit expressed by a sense of poise and security.

Sweeping the lush green fields, her gaze took in the Frisian cattle and the borderlines of water. She had grown up here, amid the dikes and silver *meers* of this watery coastal land of the Netherlands. This had always been her home, except for those few months when the angry waters of the sea, driven by some fierce spirit, came swirling in across the land. They had fled then, she and her family, traveling northeast

7

before the foaming saltwater which ate the life out of their land. The path of flight, called the Way of the Vlaming, had been used several times. But that was twenty years before, and the land was again green and lush. Stepping down from the earthen dike to a lower level, she started across the flat toward a little cottage.

But all was not peace, for North Flanders was astir with the crosscurrents of the time. Historic Ghent, capital of Flanders, was one of its largest cities. It was a major trade center of Western Europe, situated in an area rich in produce. Broad and pleasant pastures, orchards, and villages lay amid the network of fine canals which drained the land into the Lys and Schelde rivers and on to the sea.

Ghent's two hundred thousand inhabitants were governed by a senate of twenty-six elected members, subject to the Grand Council of Mechelen. Actually it covered a whole territory with its rule, composing one of the four territories of the province of Flanders. Its industry was composed of fifty-two guilds of manufacturers and thirty-two tribes of weavers. Its textile business was one of the most outstanding in Western Europe, with many weavers having been supplied to England where a rival textile industry now flourished.

No city in the Christian world, according to Erasmus, compared with Ghent for size, power, political constitution, or the culture of its inhabitants. Bells were rung daily and the drawbridges over the many arms of the river which intersected the city were raised and business suspended while the workers returned.

The city had spirit and a basic drive for freedom.

9

They had survived the aftermath of their punishment by King Charles V for their attempted insurrection. In spite of his heavy tax of 40,000 florins they had regained a good measure of prosperity. But the people had not gotten over their resentment toward the "unworthy son of Ghent," and especially his defiant act of removing the great bell Roland from its central place in the city. Its iron tongue had called the citizens to arms for centuries, and the burghers of Ghent had been as proud of Roland as of their children! Beneath the surface of the struggle for liberty was the struggle to give birth to freedom of conscience.

Having spent most of the day at the famous Ghent market, Soetgen was anxious to get home. It was later than usual, and she hurried as she neared the little grove of trees which surrounded their house. Somewhere beyond she would find her husband, Willem, and the children at the evening milking. They would be through shortly, she was sure, and she wanted to surprise them with the cuts of meat she had brought for their meal. It wasn't often that she indulged in extras, but tonight it would be lambchops, done to a turn over the hearth, with the fresh bread she had left for Betken to watch in the oven. The thought of little "Bet," handling the broad flat paddle, lifting the loaves from the long stone oven in the backyard, brought a smile to her lips.

She was aware of the fragrance of freshly baked bread as she entered the kitchen. Golden brown loaves stood in a neat row on the table. Quickly she added fuel to the warm coals in the fireplace. Tying an apron about her, she soon had the chops on the spit, swinging over the fire. The melting grease sputtered in the flame, making pleasant sounds while she worked. Setting the table with the few dishes needed for the five, she pulled Tanneken's high stool from its corner.

"Now," she thought, "let them come; it's as nearly ready as need be."

She could hear their voices and laughter as they came up the broad walk. The sound of clogs being placed on the back stoop announced their arrival, and suddenly they were upon her! The girls tugged at her apron, hopefully. David stood a bit apart, watching in the more mature reserve of his ten years. Willem put his arm around her shoulders and pressed her against himself in an expression of affection.

"It's been a long day, Soetgen. We missed you. How was the trip and the market?"

"It was fine, Wim, and I had a busy time. The docks were full of boats, and the prices were good. I had some interesting conversations. But I'll tell you later. Come, the meat is done."

They hadn't noticed the evening special in the haste of their welcome. Now with exclamations of pleasure the children hurried to the table. Lifting the spit from its hinge she placed a smoking chop on each plate. They bowed their heads in silence, each making the sign of the cross. At Willem's "Amen" the children began asking about the market and the city. While they ate, she told them of the many things on sale, of the various people she had met, and of the big cheeses that dwarfed her basket of small ones.

"But you sold them all, Mother," said David. "They must like ours."

"Yes, ours were gone in no time, and I was free to shop. New hose for you, David; a bright apron for you, Betken; and I couldn't resist a new bonnet for Tanneken!"

"You forgot me, I suppose," said Willem, a twinkle in his eye, "or did you remember my request?"

"It's right there in the basket, my lord," she added the title with a slight pause and a lift of her left brow. "I wouldn't forget the one who treats me like a queen."

Their eyes met and held for a long moment. An expression of warmth passed between them, which the children felt but didn't fully understand.

"I met Aunt Bet," she added, breaking the silence, "and she sends her greetings. She asked about you, Bet, wanting to know how her little namesake is doing. When I told her you were tending the oven today, she laughed to think of you wrestling with loaves of bread half your own size!"

After clearing the table and emptying the basket, the children were sent off to bed. Each had a bunk, built closet-wise in the wall. They scurried up short ladders to their beds and were soon fast asleep. A larger one folded out from the wall in a little room beyond them for Soetgen and Willem. They sat by the hearth, enjoying the glow of the peat fire under its film of ashes.

She and Willem had been married nearly twenty years and they were still lovers. Willem was a large man, bearing the marks of toil. Soetgen was tall, but slight beside him. While her youth was behind her, she was still lovely, even more beautiful in her maturity.

"I stopped at the cathedral, Wim, and sat in silence awhile. Of course I saw the van Eyck altarpiece. I never get tired of looking at it — one hundred years old and as beautiful as when he created it."

"You're different from me, Soet, your interest in art and the like. I'm just a working man." Willem stretched out his rough hands and looked at them as he turned them over.

Soetgen took one in hers and laughed. "But strong, Wim, strong and secure; you know what life is about. While I walked along the Lys today, and admired the design of the beautiful houses, I thought to myself, I'd rather live in our old house with my Wim than in a mansion along the Lys!"

He smiled at this, and then asked, "And what did you women talk about? I suppose," he continued, "about your husbands."

Both laughed and then grew serious. She answered, "You've spoiled me, Wim. Not many men treat their wives as companions as you treat me!"

"Perhaps not all men realize as I do what you've made of me, or they would." His voice was warm as he responded.

"Betken's Jan is so different. I actually believe she lives in fear. Not that he is mean to her, but she just doesn't have any say of her own."

"Did she talk of this again today?"

"Yes, she did. But, even more, of the Anabaptist groups who impress her with their happiness and joy."

"Anabaptists!" He fairly spat out his words. "I thought that since the fall of Münster no one would listen to them again. Those polygamists had little

13

regard for their women." His eyes flashed fire. "I can't see why their group should grow, with all their odd practices, let alone the way they're being hunted and killed. That's all we hear from Antwerp and Amsterdam — another trial, another burned at the stake or beheaded. How it has upset the peace of Ghent! A stubborn lot; we hear much about them on the canals."

Soetgen looked at him in silence for a moment. Normally a well-controlled man, his occasional outbursts of anger always gave her a sense of awe.

"You sound like my brother Hendrik, Wim. He's so hostile. He seems to hate the Anabaptists. Just today he denounced them as stupid for having women serve as leaders in some of their programs."

"That is stupid, Soet. Women ought to serve in the home and raise the children. If this keeps on the whole country will be as mixed up as the Münsterites."

"But Betken says the Anabaptists are neither Münsterites nor stubborn, but a peaceful and kind people who live as saints. They have happy homes; even death is accepted as a sacrifice to God."

"How many does she know who are like that?" he retorted.

"There are many around, as you know. The movement is spreading like grassfire. Many have accepted their baptism, even in our seigniory. So many are tired of the Church treating them as if they are less important than their few thalers! Some of our near neighbors have joined them."

"Another futile bid for freedom. We've had Waldenses, Albigenses, Perfectists, Poplicans, Brethren of the Common Life, Arnoldists, Bohemian Brothers, and now this group. If they are so interested in change, why don't they take on the Spaniards and free the Netherlands?"

"Wim, don't say such things. You might be heard!"

"I know, Soetgen, but the Spanish tyranny is such a burden, and this rebel movement only makes matters worse. It is the Spanish who enforce the Inquisition anyway."

"But the Anabaptists are not revolutionaries of that type. They are promoting a revolution of faith."

"This may be true, but they can't take on the whole religious world! The Church can't trust everyone to interpret faith."

"This is just it, Wim. The Scriptures are available to us all now. These people claim that anyone can read the Bible and understand." She paused a moment. "I wish I had a copy."

"And then what? You'll get ideas like Claes Weynken promoted at the Hague — or Willem Muliers, or van Overdam right here at Ghent? You could be burned at the stake, too, or drowned!"

She shuddered at the thought, and he reached over and took her hand.

"Soet, that's not for you. Rome isn't bothering us. Let's stay the way we are. Be satisfied with the freedom we have."

"I know, Wim, and in a way I am. But only today Betken was telling me what she has learned about Claes Weynken, about her faith and the details of her trial. That woman wasn't just a stubborn rebel. She

15

believed that she was sharing a truth the Church has crushed."

"And what truth is that?"

"Well, it's strange, but it is as if she had a faith in God that was direct, that didn't need the forms of the Church. You have said yourself, Wim, that if we have to rely on hypocritical priests to get us through to God we have a slim chance!"

"That I have, Soet, but do you think this Claes Weynken got through to God?"

"How can I know — but she gave evidence of some touch with God at her trial."

"She did?"

"Well, the way she so freely and ardently defended her faith shows that she had an understanding of her own."

"Her own, indeed! She was just plain stubborn." His ire rose.

"I don't think so, Wim. Her expressions that the sacraments are only bread and water and that the sacred oil is good for salad and boots were her way of saying that Christ is not contained in elements."

"But she rejected the Holy Church completely!"

"I know, but one has to admire her courage. And I do admire Weynken's bold confession." She was calm and earnest as she spoke.

"Her confession?" he queried.

"Yes. At her trial a monk showed her a wooden crucifix, shouting, 'Here is your Lord and your God.' She answered, 'This is not my God; the cross by which I am redeemed is a different one. This is a wooden god; throw him into the fire and warm

16

yourselves with him.' No wonder she was burned!"

Willem sat in silence, wrinkles creasing his forehead as his brows drew together in thought. "I didn't know you were discussing all this with Bet. You seem to know a lot about this movement."

"Can we avoid it, Wim? They are all around us. They meet in houses, in boats, and in the woods nearly every day. There have been arrests, imprisonments, trials, and burnings every month."

"I know, Soet. I've been thinking a lot about this," he paused, "since seeing van Overdam die."

Soetgen looked at him in amazement. He had never said a word. "Willem! You didn't tell me!"

"I know. I didn't know what to think of the horrible mess, and I didn't say anything."

"You — you mean you were there?"

"Yes, I was there. I wish I could forget it. The sight and his words continue to haunt me."

"Tell me about it, Wim," she said softly.

He began slowly, "There were two of them burned together. They led van Overdam and Hans Keeskooper down the street in the midst of a shouting mob. At the site they told the two to prepare themselves for execution. Keeskooper asked to remove his hose and sat down and started taking off his stockings. Overdam immediately began speaking to the people. The soldiers tried to help with the stockings but Keeskooper insisted on doing it alone. He took his time at it so that van Overdam could preach longer. A hush fell over the crowd, and we all listened spellbound to his last words. Finally, they burned them, and while burning the two sang with joy. . . . I can't forget it."

17

Soetgen looked at him in astonishment. After some moments she broke the silence, "They have something, Wim, and their freedom and joy is too sincere for us to ignore."

"Yes, and there have been many more. There was Gillis and Elizabeth, here in Ghent, burned together at the stake. I saw that. The executioner embarrassed her by unlacing her gown, and she stood in her shift and linen trousers they had given her in prison. It was horrible — yet they sang for joy!" He shook his head from side to side, "Fools, the lot of them, I don't understand it."

"They claim a faith, Wim, a faith of which one witnesses by baptism."

"But it's against the law. You know the decree of the emperor! Since Charles V signed it in Brussels, it has had rigorous enforcement across our Netherlands."

They sat watching the last coal of fire flicker and die. Willem reached for her hand. "Come, Soet, it's our time for bed." She picked up the candle and they paused to look at the sleeping children, then they walked together into the little room where their bed folded from the wall. Later as he slept she reviewed the day. She would need to tell him more.

2 From where he stood, Willem could see the tall graceful spire of the church of St. Jan in Ghent. Here Charles V had been baptized — much good it had done him! His gaze returned to the Lys River into which the canal at his feet emptied. He turned and walked along the path that followed the canal. In his thoughts he wished he could turn his back on the issues focused with such sharp tension in Ghent.

The clouds scudded swiftly and loosely across the heavens. In the clear patches of sky the pale golden light glimmered, casting a silver sheen on the clouds. On both sides of the canal flat fields were marked by drainage ditches and the windmills pumped water from the fields over the narrow dikes. The day was fine, the wind whipped his scarf around his neck, and the windmill's cogs creaked as the breeze forced their arms to move rapidly. His thoughts were with Soetgen as he contemplated on their questions.

Soetgen and the children were in the back field digging turnips. The cool fall weather made it cold to work in the soil, and her fingers hurt from removing the dirt. Her clogs kept sticking in the mud. David carried the baskets to the cart and hauled them to the trench near the barn. The girls followed her down the row, pulling the turnips and filling the baskets. Stored in the trench and covered with straw, then earth, they would last almost through the winter.

Today Willem was cleaning the canals, and Soetgen was alone with her thoughts. With the growing trade at Ghent the men on the canals were kept busy; he was gone from home much of the time. Ghent was prospering from the trade which moved north down the Rhine Valley. While the city didn't rival Paris in art, it certainly did in size. Ghent was now the major center of social and political activity in the north. Having become, in 1500, the birthplace of Charles V, the populace was now, half a century later, torn between desire for national freedom and pride in its prominence through his leadership. But trade was not all that moved north to Ghent — the trade routes were the carriers of information and religious influence. Anabaptists were to be found in Ghent in ever-increasing numbers.

Yesterday's conversation with Betken had stirred Soetgen deeply. She had known of the spread of the Anabaptists, and that they were condemned by the Church as heretics. If Bet was right, the Anabaptists had both an order of life and experienced a continued growth over the past twenty years. The report that in spite of persecution a leadership conference had been held at Harlingen somehow excited her. What impressed her most was that this faith was personal and responsible.

When she stopped by the old homestead to chat with her sister Nettie and their brother Hendrik she found them quite vocal in their views. Their attitude, like Wim's, was that of hostility to the movement. They too had witnessed burnings, had seen Pieter van

Olman of Ghent die, and resented the bloody mess. Their words to Soetgen were a warning, "Women don't belong in the discussions of faith; let the men take care of that."

But Betken's different words rang clearly in her ears, "Soet, you are the one who ought to be studying this movement; you're a leader; I'm only a follower."

It was true, at home Bet had always followed her. She had led in the work and the mischief, with Betken either sharing or covering for her. Now, living near Antwerp, Betken was being subjected to this influence with no one to guide her. Jan, her husband, was unconcerned and uncommunicative where matters of religion were involved. She had to find some sense of religious fellowship, and Soetgen didn't blame her for this interest. But for herself, it was different, having Wim and the children with her. What else did she need?

But this unrest stirred within her. In her quiet moments she asked herself, "What is the meaning of life, especially life for a woman?" She actually pitied some of the women she knew. Their pattern of life meant that they were little more than slaves for their men. It wasn't the nature of their work that she resented; she worked too. It was the fact that they weren't companions. They had no freedom to share as equals in experiencing together the meaning of life. "Are women less responsible than men," she pondered, "or less adept at conversation about faith?"

"Was it true," she wondered, "that this Anabaptist group provided freedom?" What all was meant by a "believers' fellowship?" She wished she could meet an Anabaptist for herself; she'd try to find out what these people were really like.

As she worked and thought, the next days passed rapidly. Fall was about gone, and the days had become shorter and gray. Today the creak of the windmill sounded labored and sullen as the sails turned in the cool wind.

Soetgen and the girls had gone to the far end of the polder to bring in a heifer and her newly born calf. The calf was still very weak; so it took extra time to bring them in. Willem was doing the milking, while they brought the animals to the stable. They tried to hurry. David would have returned from school and be helping Willem by now, and they would soon want to eat. Nearing the house, she saw Wim already coming from the cows with the pails of milk. He set the pails down and waited to open the gate for her.

At the same moment they both saw a lone figure coming across the meadow, just beyond the willows. They watched him as he approached, his hurried step broken by a limp, a walking stick in his hand, and his broad hat tilted back on his head. As he drew near, they could see his chest rise and fall with his heavy breathing.

The stranger stopped at the edge of the lot which surrounded house and barn. He raised his hand in a friendly greeting and said breathlessly, "Peace be to your house."

"And to yours," responded Willem.

The man stood in silence a moment, breathing

deeply. Obviously he was exhausted. They saw him look carefully at each member of the family. There was a bit of a smile in his eyes, almost wistful, as he looked at the children. His gaze came back to Willem and to Soetgen.

"May I be so bold as to ask for a beaker of milk and perhaps a piece of bread? As you can see, I've been on a hurried trip." He chuckled a bit as he looked down at his mud-flecked trousers.

"Of course," said Willem. "Won't you come in?"

"Thank you, sir, I'd best not. I'll drink it here, if you don't mind. Besides, it's for your good." He paused. "You see, I'm what they call an Anabaptist, and I'd not want you to suffer for kindness to me."

Soetgen heard Willem draw in his breath sharply. Her own pulse quickened. For once they were meeting one of the hated group. What should she do, feed him? She looked at Willem, his gaze fixed on the stranger; finally he turned slowly and nodded to her. Picking up one of the pails, she hurried into the house. Choosing a large mug, she poured it brimming full, got two rolls, and hurried back to the men.

The stranger was sitting on the back of the cart. He looked tired, leaning forward with his hands on his knees. He looked up from under his hat, showing a wrinkled forehead and lock of brown-gray hair, over his temple. He was a much older man than she had earlier thought. With a smile, he thanked her for the milk and bread, and then bowed his head. "Father, for Thy goodness and for these kind friends I thank Thee. Grant us each wisdom and the will to walk with Thee, in the name of our Lord. Amen."

With this he drank about a third of the mug of milk and then started eating a roll. Looking at Willem, he said, "I owe you a better introduction. I'm Menno Simons, leader of the brotherhood of the believers' church, which you have heard called heretical. There's a price of one hundred Carl-guilders on my head, as you may know, and I would not endanger your home by coming inside. Should you be asked, you did not know my name when you gave me to eat." With this he smiled as though living in danger was an everyday affair.

At their stunned silence he continued, "Just today I barely escaped with my life. That is why I arrived so exhausted. I've been running for several hours, and my feet can scarcely keep up with my heart!"

Again he chuckled, and Soetgen felt less awe and a growing interest in the man. She broke the silence this time. "You say you just escaped — were you a prisoner?"

"No, not quite, God be praised. He's delivered me so often it looks like it's getting to be His way!" He smiled good-naturedly at this and Soetgen noticed Willem's mouth relax its firm line.

He had emptied his mug, so she reached for it, asking, "May I bring you another?"

"If you can spare it, I'd be grateful; it may be all I will have for a while."

She quickly filled the glass and returned from the house. Willem was saying, "Your escape, was it something we should know?"

"I'd best tell you what happened. I was riding the canal boat toward Antwerp when I noticed horsemen

25

riding up from the south. As they came near, I could see they were commissaries and suspected they were after me. They reined up on the bank just ahead of the boat, and as we drew near, they called to the boatswain, asking if one Menno Simons was aboard. The canal wasn't too wide there and we were near the north bank, so I said to the boatman, 'You can tell them no,' and I jumped for the land and off across country as fast as I could go." He looked up with a twinkle in his eyes, "You should have heard their shouts!" Then his face grew serious.

"They'll not give up the chase, the bloodthirsty papists. They may call here. You didn't shelter me; so you are free, and you don't know where I'm going."

Willem said, "But it is late, and you can't go on."

"Oh, but I can," he said. "I've done it many times before." And his eyes grew wistful, "Away from my wife and family most of the time, to save them as well as myself. I am a man of the Way, living on the move, hated and hunted, called a heretic and a hedge-preacher, but," and here he looked at them with a fire in his eyes and a glow on his face, "I'm happier than when I was a capricious priest."

Willem looked at him almost incredulously. "You mean, sir, that you enjoy this freedom?"

"To which freedom are you referring?"

"Well, sir, the freedom to roam as you are."

"Mr. — uh?" and Menno paused with a wrinkled brow which asked the question.

"Van den Houte," Willem said. "Willem and Soetgen."

26

Menno Simons smiled, "Mr. van den Houte, roaming isn't freedom. The freedom I enjoy is an inner one. True freedom is in Christ, to live as a member of His kingdom, slave to the tyranny of no man!" His voice rang with his words.

"But," expostulated Soetgen, "your wife, your family, don't they resent this?"

"Resent it? Yes, we both have resented it, needing to be apart, always on the run — for the sake of the cause, not out of fear, for we live daringly," and here he smiled looking down at the latest marks of flight. "But," he said, resuming the conversation, "we resented it, believing that all men and women should be free to live by faith and conscience rather than by coercion."

"Then your wife," Soetgen interrupted. "She believes as you do?"

"Yes, she did, but she's gone now. Two years ago she became ill, and then passed on with the blessed ones." Here he sat in silence for a long moment, doubtless thinking of her, then added, "We are heirs together in the grace of God."

Heirs together! The words caught Soetgen's attention, and she pondered them, lost to the conversation. Suddenly his voice brought her back to the moment.

"Ours is a cross-bearing church. It is my lot to be away from those I love, to meet them only for a moment for a brief rendezvous at some secluded spot, and assure them of my love, to know that my family is watched every day in an effort to catch me coming home. This has been our lot for years and continues to be. I'm only in this area for a brief trip from Holstein, visiting our churches."

Soetgen looked at Willem and noticed that he seemed moved.

"But I must leave now," and he got to his feet, stretched his stooped frame a bit from its stiffness, and reached his hand to Willem. "I thank you, sir, for your kindness, and for listening. And perhaps we can meet again." Now he glanced at Soetgen as well. "You, too, can be heirs together of His grace."

Turning back to Willem, he said, "Visit one of our meetings; there are many around Ghent, almost daily. The city is so large that we are lost in the shuffle. We even meet in the woods, behind hedges or in the fields, or in boats on the river — anywhere we can gather. We can discuss faith freely elsewhere, here I endanger your home."

"But," said Willem, looking at the tired features of the old man, "I invited you to be our guest. It now becomes our responsibility."

"Yes," Menno answered, "true enough, but you may invite me after you've thought it over, not under the pressure of my needs at the moment. I bid you adieu, my friends, and God give you His peace."

With this he turned and started slowly across the meadow. They watched his dark figure go up the dike and then disappear into the dusk. They stood in silence until the chatter of the children caught their attention. Having entered the house, Willem took care of the milk and Soetgen spread the table. Both were strangely silent through the evening and retired early, each with his own thoughts. A different world had invaded theirs; it was impossible to ignore it.

3 The quest for truth has a way of captivating the whole mind. Once it is stimulated, nothing but truth will satisfy. The journey into one's self, into one's mind, is the longest one in life. Here no man should be a copy; each must face for himself that glow which beckons one on. So it was with Soetgen and Willem. For the next number of days there was little conversation between them regarding the visit of the Anabaptist. They had retreated individually to the world of thought to ponder this encounter. Willem had become moody much of the time and almost distant. Soetgen, in turn, was nearly bursting with curiosity to know more about this believers' fellowship.

Willem was in Ghent today. The late fall weather was cold, and he had gone to the wheat quay, the market along the river. He wasn't due back for at least an hour, yet she found herself going to the door often, looking toward the city to see if he was returning. She shivered in the cool air, watched the wind chase the fallen leaves across the path in front of the door, looked up at the low clouds threatening snow, closed the door, and placed another piece of wood on the fire. Calling Betken to watch the pot of stew, she took David and the pails and went to do the milking. Willem would be tired, but they would have much to talk about.

They wore heavy coats to break the wind. It felt good to lay her face against the warm flank of the cow as she forced the streams of milk into the pail. The milk drummed a staccato-like tone against the side of the bucket. In less than an hour they were finished and David opened the gate as she carried the pails back to the house. She strained the milk through a cloth into the large milk keg to take out every fleck of grass or dirt that had fallen off the udders of the cows. Handing David the buckets to rinse with water, she covered the keg. Now the work was done for the evening, and they would wait together for Willem's return.

"Mother," Betken asked, "what do you think is taking Father so long today?"

"He'll be here soon, I'm sure," she replied. "I think he's been talking with folks in town."

"He's been quiet lately," David remarked. "I think he's wondering about that visitor who stopped here."

"What makes you think that, David?" she asked.

"Oh, the other day we were bringing a load of grass to the cowshed, and when we were loading it on the cart, there was a hole in the stack, and Father said, 'I wonder where he slept — maybe here.' Then after a bit he added, 'Strange a man will live like this for faith.' "

Soetgen's heart leaped. Willem must be thinking thoughts similar to hers. Wrestling with her own questions, she had not recognized how much they were sharing this quest, only in isolation from each other's thoughts. True, Willem didn't think through or decide as quickly as she did, but when he came to his position, he knew why he was there, and he didn't move easily.

The sound on the stoop announced his arrival. When Willem entered, the children greeted him with a rush of pleasant expressions. He gave each in turn a warm embrace, lifted Tanneken high in the air, and then set her down on her stool at the table. "There, that's what you have all been wanting." Turning to Soetgen he put his arm around her and held her close a moment before placing her chair and seating himself. The meal was interspersed with comments about the day, with little things of interest to the family. After dinner and dishes they relaxed around the fireplace for a quiet evening.

"I heard much about these Anabaptists in the city. There are quite a few in the Ghent prison now." He paused a moment as they pondered this, then continued. "Our visitor the other day was all we thought he was, and more," he began. "I inquired about Menno Simons today. He's quite a colorful figure, one must admit."

Soetgen's hands paused over her knitting. She looked at the sweater a moment, then at Willem and said simply, "Yes?" Her voice was soft, and carried an inflection which called for more.

"This wasn't the first time he's had a narrow escape. There's another story of his cunning making the rounds. No one is quite sure whether it actually happened or not."

"What's that, Father?" David asked. He leaned forward on his stool, eager for the answer.

"It seems, son, that Menno Simons was riding on

31

a coach several years ago, before he was especially well known, but was even then being sought by the officers. A group of commissaries set up a roadblock and stopped the coach. Menno suspected they were looking for him. Quickly he swung out of the coach and greeted them courteously. 'Can we be of service, my lords?' Their curt answer was, 'We are looking for Menno Simons.' Without a moment's pause, Menno turned, put his head inside the door and asked loudly, 'Is Menno Simons in here?' Each person answered no, whereupon Menno turned to the officers saying, 'My lords, accept our apology for not being able to oblige; they say Menno Simons is not in the coach.' The men acknowledged the driver's patience for interrupting the schedule. Menno swung back into the coach and they rolled on!"

Soetgen and the children laughed heartily. "Quite smooth," David chuckled.

Willem reached over and tousled his hair. "Enough for tonight, son. Off to bed, children; Mother and I want to talk."

When they were alone, Willem said, "Menno was a priest at Witmarsum in Friesland. He served at Pingjum earlier, and according to the reports he wasn't very pious — cards, gambling, drinking, and revelry. He had a clash with the sacramentarians, and in an effort to answer them, he began studying the Scriptures. He seems to have enjoyed getting into a good controversy. But his heated debates with the Münsterites were probably a reaction because his own brother Pieter had joined them. It seems he was more and more impressed by the faith of some of the suffering Anabaptists by the way they died for what they believed. At Leeuwarden, an Anabaptist, Sicke Snijder, was burned at the stake. Menno was given a full report of the event. Deeply moved by the man's spirit and words he began studying the Scriptures for himself. Something happened to him, for in January of 1536 he left the priesthood and joined the Anabaptist people. About a year later they called him to be their leader."

"He's really not a Münsterite then?" Soetgen asked.

"No, he isn't. He disagreed with them, and the group he leads is quite different. His preaching against them while a priest led him to examine their beliefs and consequently to question his own position. He finally left the Church."

"Then Nettie and Hendrik are wrong," she said. "I was talking with them again yesterday and they think the whole group are Münsterites."

"No, they really aren't. And they are different from most of us."

"In what way, Wim?"

"Well, from what I've learned they are happy and secure. They seem to have found a purpose in life beyond just making a living."

"Yes, I felt that way about Menno. He seems to know what he is doing."

"He certainly does, and even with all the pressure he is under, he's apparently at peace."

"It has been over twenty years now that he's been in this new movement. He must be satisfied," Soetgen added. "He seemed quite sure of himself when he was here the other evening."

After a few moments of silence Willem spoke hesitantly, "Soet, I wish we could find a more satisfying faith; ours is nothing but a shell. Indulgences and masses don't offer much by way of inner peace."

As she looked at him, tears came to her eyes. "Oh, Wim, I didn't know you felt that way. I've also had a hunger for something better."

"I've known, Soet. Did you think I didn't understand why you always talked religion at the market?"

"Yes, I've been searching for more than religious performance. Ever since I've read Thomas a Kempis' *Imitation of Christ*, I've been troubled."

"I thought for a while you were going to ask me to join the Brethren of the Common Life!"

She blushed, then said, "Perhaps that would have been easier; now we don't know where to turn."

"Well, we might visit one of Menno's meetings," he commented. "We can't ignore his faith when he shares it right at our door."

4 Faith has a way of unfolding, slowly but surely, in response to evidence. Through the short winter days and long evenings Soetgen and Willem had time to talk and reflect. They went about their duties with a longing to know more of the happenings that were changing their lives. They listened to the talk of others as they went to and from Ghent on the frozen canal. Like glittering ribbons of ice the canals became roadways in the winter. The trees and bushes became a fairyland when covered with hoarfrost. The winter scene spangled each crystal with gold, and the exhilaration kissed each traveler with a touch of ecstasy. Yet in their inner thoughts there was a constant yearning for something more.

The political changes were more oppressive rather than less. Charles V had abdicated the Netherlands to his son Philip II, in October 1555, in royal ceremonies at Brussels. Amidst the splendor of his entourage and the glory of the Knights of the Golden Fleece, burghers and senators knelt and swore allegiance to the young king.

Now, in the city of Ghent, tension hung heavily over the populace. The edict of Charles V was being vigorously reasserted by Philip II, King of Spain. Charles V had at least come from Flanders and had some personal identification with the Flemish. Now Philip II, born and educated in Spain, a truly Spanish man, gave new directives to magistrates in the Spanish-occupied countries. His marriage in 1554 to Mary Tudor, queen of England, had not made him more tolerant. Enforcing the Inquisition he sought to exterminate all Protestants, justifying his severity by saying that he was carrying out the edict long before enacted by his father. The decrees of Ghent were circulated and posted across the city. Persons who failed to conform to the demands of the Holy Church were to be crushed, in whatever manner necessary, and their property confiscated for the emperor. He had two great machines to enforce his rule, the Court of Mechelen and the Inquisition.

As yet the van den Houtes had not visited an Anabaptist meeting. But one day Soetgen had learned at the market in Ghent that a group was meeting the following evening at a neighbor's house. Comments about the meeting were passed among the market folk with a sense of expectancy. The excitement got to her, almost as an undercurrent. From the conversation it was clear that they were talking of more than one meeting. Gatherings were being held in various homes in the community almost daily.

There was some speculation that Menno Simons would be in the area this week. Others were speaking excitedly of Leenaert Bouwens. He was known as a strong leader, recently converted to the movement. A persuasive speaker, he was highly regarded by people in the lower Waterland region. It was said that already he had baptized more into the believers' church than any other leader.

Soetgen hurried home through the cold afternoon,

anxious to share the news with Willem. She had determined to go to the meeting. There was no peace as long as one lived in uncertainty. She had reviewed again and again the shallow pretense of their own religion, of the forms that meant so little in actual life. It was evident that she and Willem had no faith to talk about. Their lives held little meaning beyond what they gave each other. Perhaps they could yet find a real purpose for life. She asked herself, "What actually is the meaning of the freedom she had so often talked about? Was it something other than what she understood?" Again the words used by Menno ran through her mind, "Heirs together of the grace of God."

When she told him, Willem was ready to attend the meeting. He laughed anxiously, and said, "The rolling sea is not to be stopped by a basketful of earth!" He sensed that this new movement of faith was like a floodtide, sweeping across the lowlands. In spite of all their caution they too were being caught up in it. The laugh was only on the surface, for before they left, he looked long at the little ones, then asked, "And what of these? Are we endangering them?"

"But," she responded, "if we do not find the answer, what have we to give them?"

He nodded his head. "What is truly for our good should be for theirs as well."

With a parting word to David about their bedtime, they were off. The snow and wind whipped around them as they walked, stifling conversation. It was dusk when they arrived at the neighbor's home. From outside there was little light showing from the windows.

"Perhaps we're mistaken," Willem said. "It doesn't appear that there is a gathering here."

"But the windows are closed, Wim; they hide the meeting."

He rapped on the door with the back of his hand. In a moment it was opened a crack and a man's deep voice said, "Yes?"

"Is there a meeting here that we might attend tonight? We are the van den Houtes from across the field."

"And how am I to know of your sympathy if I'm to trust letting you in?"

Willem looked at Soetgen for a moment. She was the one who had learned of the meeting in town. Suddenly she said, "Menno Simons is one of your leaders. We are friends of his."

The door opened, and the man reached out his hand. "That's good enough. We can't be too careful. You see, he is here tonight. I'm Hans Timmerman. We're glad to have you."

They were led through the main room of the house to the kitchen. A door led into a large room beyond used for the farmer's milk and cheese. As the door was opened they could hear the soft tones of a group singing.

Mr. Timmerman pointed them to several stools just inside. A small group of some thirty people was packed into the room. At the front sat Menno Simons. He looked old and tired tonight, yet a soft smile lifted the corners of his mouth as he surveyed the group. They weren't sure whether he recognized them in the candlelight or not.

The music was familiar, a tune Soetgen had often heard on the canals and at the market. But the words were different — not the ones she knew of the popular feeling for the homeland, but the story of some man of faith. She'd have to ask about him later, a Michael Sattler who had perished in the flames for his faith in Holy Writ. There was an atmosphere of intense feeling as they sang, as though they were identifying with the martyr in his death.

The song ended, and Menno began to speak.

You are here because you wish to be saved. The Scripture is clear that by all means, first of all, your earthly, carnal life must be reformed.

It is true repentance that the Scriptures teach and enjoin upon us, with admonitions, threatenings, reprovings, miracles, examples, ceremonies, and sacraments. If you do not repent, there is nothing in heaven or on earth that can help you, for without true repentance we are comforted in vain. The prophet Isaiah says, O my people, they which lead thee cause thee to err, and destroy the way of thy paths.

Furthermore, we must be born from above, must be changed and renewed in our hearts. We must be transplanted from the unrighteous and evil nature of selfishness into the true and good nature of Christ. Without this transformation we can never in all eternity be saved by any means, be they human or divine. Wherever these two, true repentance and the new creature, are not . . .

Here he paused and looking kindly at several younger children before him, remarked, "I speak of those who are of the age of understanding."

Then fixing his gaze again on the group continued,

there, man must be eternally lost. This is incontrovertibly clear. This everyone who does not wish to deceive his soul may very properly store in the little box of his conscience!

This regeneration of which I speak, from which comes the penitent, pious life that has the promise, can only originate in the Word of the Lord, rightly taught and rightly understood and received in the heart by faith through the Holy Ghost.

The first birth of man is out of the first and earthly Adam, and therefore its nature is earthly and Adam-like. Man is carnally minded, unbelieving, disobedient, and blind to divine things; deaf and foolish; whose end, if not renewed by the Word, will be damnation and eternal death. If you desire to have your perverse nature cleared up, and desire to be free from eternal death and damnation so that you may obtain with all true Christians that which is promised them, then you must be born again. It is the regenerate who are in grace and have the promise as you have heard.

The regenerate lead a penitent and new life, for they are renewed in Christ and have received a new heart and spirit. Once they were earthly minded, now heavenly; once they were carnal, now spiritual; once they were unrighteous, now righteous; once they were evil, now good. They live no longer after the old corrupted nature of the first earthly man, but after the new upright nature of the new and heavenly Man, Christ Jesus. It is as Paul says: Nevertheless, I live; yet not I, but Christ liveth in me. Their poor, weak life they daily renew more and more, and that after the image of Him who created them. Their minds are like the mind of Christ. They gladly walk as He walked. They crucify and tame their flesh with all its evil lusts.

In baptism such bury their sins in the Lord's death and rise with Him to a new life. They circumcise their hearts with the Word of the Lord. They are baptized with the Holy Ghost into the spotless, holy body of Christ, as obedient members of His church, according to the true

40

ordinance and Word of the Lord. They put on Christ and manifest His spirit, nature, and power in all their conduct. They fear God with all the heart and seek in all their thoughts, words, and works, nothing but the praise of God and the salvation of their beloved brethren.

Here Menno's voice was heavy with emotion. His eyes glistened in the lamplight, wet with tears. His voice took on a tone of earnestness and compassion as he continued:

I admonish and entreat you, as one who loves your soul, to repent. Repent, as I have said, without delay. The first Gospel says, The ax is laid unto the root of the trees; therefore, every tree which bringeth not forth good fruit is hewn down, and cast into the fire. Be vigilant for your poor souls that have been bought with a precious price! Be comforted no longer with open lies nor fed with husks which swine eat. I tell you in Christ, there is nothing under heaven that can or will endure before God but the new creature, faith which works by love, and the keeping of the commandments — let the learned ones clamor and write as long as they please.

My faithful hearers, do not believe me but rather the Word, to which by the grace of God I have with my small talents pointed you. I tell you, as the Lord liveth, all who teach otherwise than we have shown from the Word of the Lord, whosoever they be, are prophets who deceive you. They place pillows under your arms and cushions under your heads. They daub the wall with deceptive plaster and speak peace to the wicked, but not out of the mouth of the Lord. For as it is certain that the regenerate and penitent are the true Christians, who have God's truth, the true light, the pardon of their sins, and the sure promise of eternal life; so also it is certain that the sensuous and impenitent are false Christians, have the lies of the serpent, darkness, sin still their own, and the

41

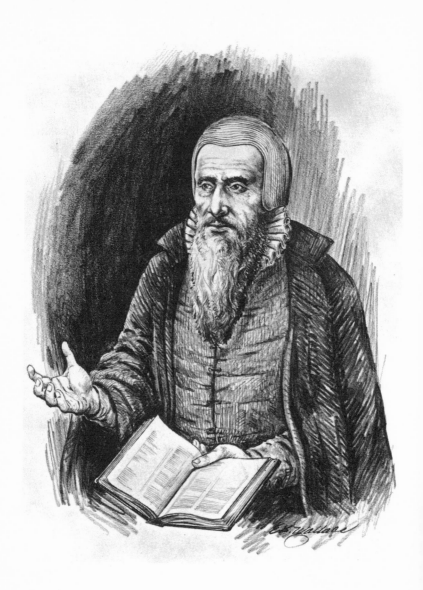

certain promise of eternal death. That this is the truth will be found to be the case in eternity before the great and Almighty God. Of this His sure Word is to me a true witness. Of this I am by His grace wholly certain.[*]

There was a hush in the room as he closed his address. His intensity gripped them, the force of his words convicted them, and yet his personal touch made them well aware that he was speaking to them in love. He folded his hands, looked up toward the ceiling, and began to pray:

May the merciful, gracious Father, through His loving Son, Christ Jesus, our Lord, grant to each the gift and grace of His Holy Spirit, so that all may hear these our Christian labors and service of true love, with such hearts as will strive for, confess, believe, and follow after the pure truth with the whole soul, and be eternally saved.

As he prayed, it seemed to Soetgen as though he was talking to Someone right in the room. His manner was so simple and personal. A feeling of conviction rested upon her as he prayed for those "who know not the Christ and His Spirit. . . ." Her attention came back to his closing words,

O Lord, Father of all grace, be pleased to open the eyes of each hearer so that they may see Thy way, Word, truth, and will, and walk therein with faithful hearts. Amen.

Following his prayer they sat in silent thought. Soetgen was thinking over what she had just heard.

[*]This quotation is adapted from selections from "The New Birth" in *The Complete Writings of Menno Simons*, edited by John Christian Wenger. Copyright 1956 by Mennonite Publishing House, Scottdale, Pa. Selections are taken from pages 92, 93, 96.

Suddenly his voice broke into her thoughts. "I'll be staying here tonight. If any of you want to talk with me, I'm available."

Willem reached over and took her hand. As she glanced at him, his eyes were fixed on Menno's. She knew he wanted to stay and sensed that his feelings were as deep as hers.

The group shared informally, becoming acquainted with one another. There seemed to be little or no hesitancy to be identified. After a brief time persons began leaving, several at a time. Soetgen and Wim made their way to where Menno was sitting.

His eyes lit up in recognition. "Ah, my friends, you did decide to visit one of our meetings."

"Yes, we did, sir, after much thought," Willem replied.

"I've prayed for this," Menno responded, "but it has taken a few months before we've seen an answer. You folks seem to be extra cautious!" He smiled knowingly.

"We are, sir, we want to be sure," Soetgen added. He nodded his head in agreement, his glance taking in both of them.

"I'm glad you are cautious. This is an important matter. Do you want to talk further tonight, or shall one of us call on you?"

"Could you?" Willem asked, "Stop at our home, I mean."

"If you would like, one of our group will do so."

With this agreement the van den Houtes excused themselves and hurried home to the children. They walked across the snow-covered meadow. Beyond them the wide arms of the windmill turned inkily black against the heavens. Above there was a canopy of stars, broken only by a sickle moon in the velvet-dark sky. They paused by the mill and Willem stood with his arm about her. She reached up and placed a cool hand on his face and drew it against her own. They were as much in love as when they were first married.

The cool air chilled them, and they hurried on to the house and to their children. All three were sleeping soundly; so they sat and talked a while before retiring. Excited about the evening experience, they looked at each other in a new light, sharing together their new insights into the Christian faith. This was the first time they had heard an Anabaptist so passionately express the faith that guided them. Impressed by the reality of faith and life in the group, they felt their own religious patterns quite empty. Anxious to find the answer to their own quest, they shared even in this moment a new wave of happiness.

5

Spring came early with its lush beauty. Soetgen gathered bunches of lavender-pink Pentecost flowers near the windmill in the meadow. Later she planted the garden and Willem toiled in the fields. This morning she was in the kitchen while Willem was at the barn helping a heifer to calve. She finished kneading the bread. Her hands were sticky with dough, and flour streaked her face. She paused with her hands on the table, deep in a world of thought.

What was their next step? What more did they need to know? What would happen to them if they joined the believers' church? If they left the State Church for this gathering of heretics? She wrung her hands together. Who was really a heretic? Did faith need to become a personal matter? Who decided the questions of faith, professionals in the study of religion or each individual for himself?

As the days passed into summer, Soetgen and Willem were visited not once, but several times. They learned much about the believers' church and about their faith. Again and again they visited meetings.

Increasingly the political forces sought to crush the heretics. An appeal to the emperor had secured some mitigation, yet by secret stimulation persecution of the movement was intensified. At Ghent the review of arrests and deaths was now a weekly occurrence. While

46

some were burned at the stake, more were beheaded, and numerous women were either drowned or buried alive. One of the more barbarous executions caused an intense reaction on the part of the public against the magistrates. A young boy, named David, and Levina, a mother of six, were bound to stakes, powder tied around their necks and they were burned. When the boy's body was seen to move the executioner thrust a pitchfork into his bowels three times, but his head still moved, so the executioner put a chain around his neck and pulled it around the stake until the boy's neck was broken. The crowd jeered the bailiff and executioner until the cries signaled an open revolt. The bailiff and his associates fled to the city hall and the bodies were removed for burial. Soetgen and Willem were now sure that this movement was the way of truth even though it was labeled heresy.

At the market pamphlets by Anabaptist leaders were continually circulated. Soetgen secured a booklet by Menno Simons, *Foundation of Christian Doctrine*, and read it with care. As its meaning became clear she discussed it at length with Willem. It was Menno's treatise on Christian discipleship. It helped them understand what the decisive issue of this new approach to faith actually was.°

We teach in the first place that which Jesus the teacher from heaven, the mouth and word of the Most High God

°The following citations are adapted from selections from "Foundation of Christian Doctrine" in *The Complete Writings of Menno Simons*, edited by John Christian Wenger. Copyright 1956 by Mennonite Publishing House, Scottdale, Pa. Selections are taken from pages 108-111, 117, 120-122.

taught (John 3:2), that now is the time of grace, a time to awake from the sleep of our ugly sins, and to be of an upright, converted, renewed, contrite, and penitent heart. Now is the time to sincerely lament before God our past reckless and willful manner of life, and in the fear of God to crucify and mortify our wicked, sinful flesh and nature. Now is the time to arise with Christ in a new, righteous, and penitent existence. Christ says, The time is fulfilled, and the kingdom of God is at hand: repent and believe the gospel.

Alas, it is time to awake! Remember the angel of Revelation has sworn by the eternal and living God who made heaven and earth that after this time, there shall be time no more. From the Scriptures we cannot conclude but that this is the last festival of the year, the last proclamation of the holy Gospel, the last invitation to the marriage of the Lamb, which is to be celebrated, published, and sanctified before the great and terrible day of the Lord. With it, it seems, the summer will pass away and the winter come forth. They who, like the foolish virgins, neglect to prepare their lamps will come too late, knock in vain, and be excluded. Therefore comfort not one another with senseless comfort and uncertain hope, as some do who think that the Word can be taught and observed without the cross.

I have in mind those who know the Word of the Lord, but do not live according to it. Oh, no! it is the Word of the cross and will in my opinion remain that unto the end. This Word has to be declared with much suffering and sealed with blood. The Lamb is slain from the foundation of the world! He did not only suffer in His members, but also by way of the cross and death has entered into that glory which He, for a time had left for our sakes. If the Head had to suffer such torture, anguish, misery, and pain, how shall His servants, children and members expect peace and freedom as to their flesh? If they have called the master of the house Beelzebub, why not those of his

48

household? All that will live godly in Christ Jesus, says Paul, shall suffer persecution. Christ says, Ye shall be hated of all men for my name's sake.

In the second place we exhort you with Christ: Repent ye, and believe the Gospel. O faithful Word of grace, O faithful Word of divine love, thou art read in books, sung in hymns, preached with the mouth as to life and death, proclaimed in many countries, but unwanted in thy power. And what is more, all those who rightly teach and receive thee are made free booty for all.

Ah, dear sirs, it will not help a fig to be called Christians, boast of the Lord's blood, death, merits, grace, and Gospel, so long as we are not converted from this wicked, immoral, and shameful life. It is in vain that we are called Christians, that Christ died, that we are born in the day of grace, and baptized with water, if we do not walk according to His law, counsel, admonition, will, and command and are not obedient to His Word.

Therefore, awake, and observe how men live everywhere. Verily you see nothing anywhere but unnatural carousing and drinking, pride as that of Lucifer, lying, fraud, grasping avarice, hatred, strife, adultery, fornication, warring, murder; everywhere hypocrisy, patent blasphemy, idolatry, and false worship. In short, nothing but a mighty opposition to all that God teaches and commands. Who can tell the terrible and alarming nature of this present world? Still men want to be called the holy Christian church. Oh, no! They who do such things, saith Paul, shall not inherit the kingdom of God.

Gentlemen, awake and beware, for the mouth of the Lord says, Verily, verily, I say unto you, Except ye be born from above, ye shall not see the kingdom of God. Also, Verily, verily, I say unto thee, Except a man be born of water and the Spirit, he cannot enter into the kingdom of God. Verily, I say unto you, Except ye be converted, and become as little children, ye shall not enter into the kingdom of heaven. What does it profit to speak much of

Christ and His Word, if we do not believe Him, and refuse to obey His commandments?

Again I say, awake and tear the accursed unbelief with its unrighteousness from your hearts, and commence a pious, penitent life as the Scriptures teach. Christ says, Except ye repent ye shall all likewise perish. Do not apply this to such repentance as is taught and practiced by a world that has lost its way, such is only in outward appearance and human righteousness, such as hypocritical fastings, pilgrimages, praying and reading many Pater Nosters and Ave Marias, hearing frequent masses, going to confessionals, and like hypocrisies — things of which Christ and His holy apostles did not say a single word and therefore cannot be a propitiatory sacrifice. Such things will be a provocation rather to stir up divine displeasure. These are empty and vain commandments of men, the accursed and magic wine of the Babylonian harlot, which those who have dwelt upon the earth have drunk for so many centuries, inviting the just anger of God.

We are referring to a penitence possessed of power and works. It is as John the Baptist taught: Bring forth therefore fruits meet for repentance, and think not to say within yourselves, we have Abraham to our Father. And now also the axe is laid unto the root of the trees; every tree, therefore, which bringeth not forth good fruit is hewn down and cast into the fire.

Finally, we say, humble yourselves in the name of Jesus, that your poor souls may be excused. Examine, I say, our doctrine, and you will find through the grace of God that it is the pure and unadulterated doctrine of Christ, the holy Word, the Word of eternal peace, the Word of eternal truth, the Word of divine grace, the Word of our salvation, the invincible Word, against which no gates of hell shall ever prevail; the two-edged sword that proceeds out of the mouth of the Lord, the sword of the Spirit by which all must be judged that dwell upon the earth.

O dear sirs, sheathe your sword. For as the Lord liveth you do not fight against flesh and blood, but against Him whose eyes are as a flame of fire; who judgeth and contends in righteousness; who is crowned with many crowns; whose name no one knoweth but Himself; who is clothed with the vesture dipped in blood; whose name is the Word of God; who rules the nations with a rod of iron; who treads the winepress of the fierceness and wrath of almighty God; who hath on His vesture and on His thigh a name written, King of kings and Lord of lords.

Christ, after His resurrection, commanded His apostles saying, Go ye therefore, and teach all nations, baptizing them in the name of the Father, and of the Son, and the Holy Ghost; teaching them to observe all things whatsoever I have commanded you; and lo, I am with you always, even unto the end of the world. Amen.

Here we have the Lord's commandment concerning baptism, as to when according to the ordinance of God it shall be administered and received; namely, that the Gospel must first be preached, and then those baptized who believe it. Christ says: Go ye into all the world, and preach the gospel to every creature; he that believeth and is baptized shall be saved, but he that believeth not, shall be damned.' Thus has the Lord commanded and ordained; therefore, no other baptism may be taught or practiced forever. The Word of God abideth forever.

Young children are without understanding and unteachable; therefore baptism cannot be administered to them without perverting the ordinance of the Lord, misusing His exalted name, and doing violence to His Holy Word. In the New Testament no ceremonies for infants are enjoined, for it treats both in doctrines and sacraments with those who have ears to hear and hearts to understand. Even as Christ commanded so the holy apostles also taught and practiced, as may be plainly perceived in many parts of the New Testament. Peter said, Repent and be baptized every one of you in the name of Jesus Christ for the remission of sins, and ye shall receive the gift of the Holy Ghost. And Philip said to the eunuch, If thou believest with all thine heart, thou mayest. Faith does not follow from baptism, but baptism follows from faith.

This then is the Word and will of the Lord, that all who hear and believe the Word of God shall be baptized. Thereby such profess their faith and declare that they will henceforth live not according to their own will, but according to the will of God. For the testimony of Jesus they are prepared to forsake their homes, possessions, lands, and lives and to suffer hunger, affliction, oppression, persecution, the cross and death for the same. Yes, they desire to bury the flesh with its lusts and arise with Christ to newness of life. Paul says: Know ye not that so many of us as were baptized into Christ Jesus were baptized into his death? Therefore we are buried with him in baptism into death; that like as Christ was raised up from the dead by the glory of the Father, even so we also should walk in newness of life.

The matter of a personal conversion troubled them.

"Wim, I have never had an experience of faith like this, for myself I mean."

"Nor have I, Soet; my parents had me baptized as a babe in arms, but I have no memory of a changed life."

"He seems so assured of salvation, as though a conversion lets the assurance of salvation rest within you rather than in the rites of the church."

"The character of this new life doesn't appear very easy! A life of suffering, bearing Christ's cross, rejecting the sword or violence — I'd have some trouble with that."

"Yes, Wim, I suppose you would, but what has the

sword ever brought to man but violence, death, and broken homes?''

"Soet, you sound like a convert already!"

They both laughed a bit apprehensively and became silent. But in the days that followed the conviction grew that they needed to surrender their lives to Christ, receive baptism, and be His disciples. One test, emphatically stressed by Menno, kept penetrating their thoughts, "Other foundation can no man lay than that is laid, which is Jesus Christ." The spirit of the group amazed Soetgen and Willem and convinced them that this faith was real, that they should join the believers' church.

Several weeks passed after they had been convinced that the faith of this movement was the faith of the New Testament. They still had not joined. The increased persecution by the State Church and the opposition of Soetgen's family made them hesitant. Within, however, they felt like traitors to their new faith in waiting to declare themselves.

Meetings were held almost daily around Ghent, and they attended meetings frequently. At times they went together but often separately. In Ghent itself a large congregation often met in the wool mill. There it was not easily detected, for people were constantly coming and going. Attending individually, while traveling to or from the market, they had little fear of being detected. But day by day as they shared their new faith in Christ, the question of open confession was before them.

Soetgen finally voiced the question, "When shall we ask for baptism, Wim?"

His ready answer almost startled her, "Any time, Soet. We know our Lord now, and we ought to be sharing His work."

And so that day she began to make plans. At the flower market she learned that Leenaert Bouwens was to be in Ghent during the next few days. He would administer the sign of baptism, she was sure, knowing his reputation in the work. She now waited for evening to discuss this with Willem.

But he had news as well which they shared after dinner. "Today I learned of plans for baptism at the Alewijns on the canal," he said. "It's to be day after tomorrow. It is thought that Leenaert Bouwens will be here and they are spreading the word."

He had been plowing the meadow that day, alone with his thoughts. Only the scraping of the plowshare and the cry of the gulls as they followed the newly turned earth had broken the quiet. A neighbor had come by to tell him of the planned baptism. He had pondered this during the day, and he had come to a decision.

Soetgen caught her breath. This was it. The time had come. Suddenly she burst out, "Wim, I want to be baptized; this must be our time."

He reached over and took her hand. "Yes, my dear, I know how you feel, I've known for some time, and I'm ready to join you!"

"We'll go together, Wim, and take the children to witness — we'll confess our faith together before them so they'll understand when it comes their turn."

"That we will," he responded. "We must stand together in Christ. Life is so different for me, Soet, since

54

I know Him. I was a wandering soul before, but I've found myself in His grace."

"I know, Wim, you're different . . . like a new man. And I think I am too," she added a bit shyly.

"You are indeed, my dearest, not that you weren't great before . . . the finest wife in the land," and he squeezed her hand, "but somehow you are more secure, more composed, and more understanding of life. Others seem to matter in a different way. Christ has made you free — to be yourself."

"Thank you, Wim, I want to live by His way."

Willem opened the lower cupboard door, picked up their copy of the Bible and handed it to Soetgen. They had not come by this easily; it had taken weeks to save enough to buy it. Even so, a Bible cost only five crowns now compared to five hundred when they had to be hand-copied.

"Read something, Soet, from His words. I wish I could read as well as you do, but I don't mind listening."

She opened the book to the Gospel of John and began to read softly from chapter 15:

> I am the true vine, and my Father is the husbandman. Every branch in me that beareth not fruit he taketh away; and every branch that beareth fruit, he purgeth it, that it may bring forth more fruit. Now ye are clean through the word which I have spoken unto you.
>
> Abide in me, and I in you. As the branch cannot bear fruit of itself, except it abide in the vine; no more can ye, except ye abide in me. I am the vine, ye are the branches. He that abideth in me, and I in him, the same bringeth forth much fruit: for without me ye can do nothing. If a man abide not in me, he is cast forth as a branch, and is

withered; and men gather them, and cast them into the fire, and they are burned. If ye abide in me, and my words abide in you, ye shall ask what ye will, and it shall be done unto you. Herein is my Father glorified, that ye bear much fruit; so shall ye be my disciples.

As the Father hath loved me, so have I loved you: continue ye in my love. If ye keep my commandments, ye shall abide in my love; even as I have kept my Father's commandments, and abide in his love. These things have I spoken unto you, that my joy might remain in you, and that your joy might be full. This is my commandment, That ye love one another as I have loved you.

When she had finished reading, they bowed their heads and Willem began to pray.

"Master, we have confessed You to each other, we believe in You, and mean to follow You. Give us of Your good and gracious Spirit for guidance and strength to obey. Go before and arrange the plans for us to share our faith in baptism. As we share this sign, may it be in sincere faith in Christ. Amen."

It was two days later that the van den Houte family joined others at Hans Alewijns' home. The house was situated on the bank of the canal, the water reaching to the stoop. The group gathered between the house and the stable for a brief exhortation before the baptism.

Leenaert Bouwens was a commanding figure, tall and blond, with blue eyes which seemed to sparkle as he surveyed the group. His words flowed with eloquent freedom. Soetgen found herself caught up in the spirit of his presentation. As she glanced at Willem, she realized that he was as deeply involved.

Bouwens' voice was clear and earnest.

"Baptism is a witness, a sign, of your faith in Jesus Christ. It is not the sacrament which saves. You are saved only by faith in Christ, a faith which trusts all to Him, a faith which obeys Him, a faith which makes you His disciple. Today we gather here to affirm this faith, to say before our fellows that we belong to Christ.

"This baptism which I administer is only a baptism with water. The Christ whom we confess as Lord baptizes with the Holy Spirit. Let your baptism here today be a testimony of your break with the old life and of your purpose to walk with Christ, of your faith and desire to receive the Holy Spirit."

Here he paused and looked over the group of nearly forty people.

"Let those of you who so share this faith and who purpose to live as new creatures in Christ present yourselves for baptism."

There was a stir in the gathering as from here and there persons moved forward to stand before Bouwens. Soetgen and Willem walked to the front and stood silently with the others.

Addressing the group, Bouwens began. "Today you present yourselves to be baptized into His church. The decision for this act is your own adult response of belief. This step is not made under a momentary encouragement from this meeting but under the call and conviction of the Spirit. I ask you each, Do you purpose to break from all in your past life which is outside the will of Christ, and confessing Him as Lord purpose to walk in obedience to His Word and Spirit?"

Each in turn answered. Soetgen's voice followed the others, resolutely affirming, "I do."

Bouwens stepped into the edge of the water, reached out his hand to the first one in the group, and led him into the water. The water was not deep here, scarcely coming to the knees.

"You will kneel to receive baptism." Leenaert's voice was solemn and low. Quietly the man knelt in the water and bowed his head. "Upon confession of your faith in Christ, which you have witnessed here in the assembly of believers. . . ."

Here Leenaert stooped, cupped his hands together to form a bowl, and raised them full of water above the bowed head. Pouring it in a small stream upon the head, he continued, "I baptize you with water in the name of the Father, of the Son, and of the Holy Spirit. May He who baptizes with the Spirit, of which this baptism with water is a symbol, give you that inner presence for newness of life. May He free you from your past life by sharing Christ's cross and may He grant you newness of life in the power of His resurrection."

So it went with each in turn, until it was Willem and then Soetgen. She had watched with tears of joy as Willem was baptized, and now she found herself kneeling in the water. Her long skirt spread out about her on its surface. The water was cool at first, then she no longer noticed it. This was her baptism, by her own choice, one that she would remember as her own, a covenant with God!

Suddenly she felt very calm . . . her heart was no longer pounding in excitement. It was as though God had put His hand upon her soul with the hush of His presence. A deep sense of awe and satisfaction filled her as she felt the water pouring onto her head and heard the words, "In the name of the Father, of the Son, and of the Holy Spirit."

As she came out of the water, Willem took both her hands in his to help her. They stood smiling into each other's eyes. She knew that he felt as deeply as she did — it was almost like their marriage over again. They were starting a new life together!

Leenaert now led the way into the house. Those who had just been baptized were given seats around a little stove where the burning wood was shedding its warmth to dry them. The children sat on the floor at the edge of the room, observing their parents quietly.

"Before we separate today," he began, "we shall share the communion of the Lord's table for the first time with these who join us in faith. By eating and drinking together, we witness to our common faith in Him."

Someone handed him a plate with bread. He held it for a moment, lifted his eyes, and prayed, "As our Lord, on the night of His betrayal, took bread and blessed it, brake it and gave it to His disciples, symbolizing the suffering He was to share in procuring our salvation, so bless us now as we break bread in the witness of our devotion to Him and participation in His suffering."

With this brief prayer, he took the loaf, broke it in two, and began passing the tray. Each in turn broke a piece from the loaf, waiting silently until all had taken, then together they ate. There was a sense of awe about what they were doing that gripped Soetgen as she looked into the faces of others. "Witnessing together of our faith in Christ," she thought, "and of our sharing His suffering."

Next Leenaert lifted the chalice of wine that had been brought. "In like manner our Lord took the cup, blessed it, and gave to the disciples, saying, Drink ye all from it, this is the new covenant in my blood."

He lifted the chalice and prayed, "Our Lord, as we drink, make us not only mindful of Your death for our salvation but of our participation in suffering for the salvation of others. Help us to own Thee as our Lord, even to the death."

Passing the cup to the first, he repeated references to the meaning of the cup as each drank. Soetgen listened to his words as she lifted it to her lips. "Jesus said, this is the new covenant, in my blood, which is shed for you."

As she handed it to Willem, her hand lingered a moment, arrested by the next words. "Are you able to drink this cup, and to be baptized with the baptism that I am baptized with, a baptism of rejection and suffering?"

Her eyes met those of Willem over the chalice, and then she released it and watched as he drank, and passed it on.

The meeting was over. The group visited briefly, planning their next meeting, and then began separarating one or two at a time rather than in a large group. Soetgen invited them to meet in their home the following Thursday. Gathering the children, who had watched the events in silence, she and Willem started off on their journey home.

For a while they remained silent as they walked, each involved with their own thoughts. As they neared home, Willem reached over and took her hand. Looking up with a smile, she noted the seriousness of his expression.

"What is it, Wim? Are you not satisfied with what we've done?"

"I've never been more so, my Soet, but this step has not been made lightly, you know, and we've yet to discover the cost."

"I'm sure of that, Wim, but we'll face that a day at a time."

"If it was only myself to be concerned about, I'd not mind so much, but you, and the children," he added, looking at the three running ahead of them.

"But we're in it together, and I've never been more satisfied." She pressed his hand lightly.

"I know, Soet. I can tell it. You're free in your spirit in spite of the dangers in our decision."

The words hung between them a few moments as they reached the last dike before the house. Pausing to rest, they could see the waterway's gleam in the setting sun. To the west a sliver of moon appeared above the windmill. The soft tinkle of a bell came to them from the cows grazing in the lush grass of the polder. The arms of the windmill were still in the quiet evening, their outline forming a luminous cross against the sky.

She took his arm and they started on. Everything seemed so peaceful about them; it was strange to speak of danger. Yet they knew the threat was real, for it was estimated that the Inquisition had killed forty thousand under Charles V alone, and now Philip II was asking that the edict be enforced. They were prime subjects for the Inquisition if caught, for the edict forbade private assemblies for devotion, the reading of Scripture within one's own doors, and the interpretation of Scripture by other than the official clergy. Soetgen broke the silence: "If it is dangerous, what more noble example could we set before our little ones, Wim? Better, even if we live short lives in true freedom, than that we should live long in bondage of spirit."

6 Joy is a matter of spirit, and the van den Houtes were constantly amazed at how different life had become for them. The children caught the spirit of their new faith, even if they didn't understand it. Their attitudes reflected their approval of their parents' happiness. Having identified with the gatherings of believers in their region, Soetgen and Willem found themselves readily included in the fellowship and responsibilities of congregational life.

In the midst of increased arrests the congregations continued to grow. It was as though the opposition called more attention to the faith of the martyrs. Now that Philip II had followed his father as king of Spain in 1556, the Inquisition was more open and aggressive. In fact, the monastic ingenuity in Flanders revived and expanded the methods of punishment used earlier on the Waldenses. They would establish guilt by a forced confession under the hot iron, hot plowshare, or boiling kettle. Then they would strip the prisoner, bind him to a stake, flay him from neck to navel, and loose swarms of bees to torture him to death. But the human conscience will not remain silent before injustice, and the decrees published in Ghent awakened sympathy for the Anabaptists. Many people responded to the call of the brotherhood for conversion to Christ. Multitudes were leaving the Holy Roman Church and joining the new movement.

Yet every group has its problems, for men of faith are also human. It soon became apparent that commitment to the authority of the Scripture did not answer all the questions. There were differences of opinion on the meaning of Scripture for the orders of the common life.

In his preaching Leenaert Bouwens was emphasizing the necessity of a disciplined congregation. He described the church as a visible expression of the people of God. As such it was to be a pure church. Both he and Menno Simons emphatically rejected the idea of the invisible church, a view held by the reformers about them. "To regard the church as invisible, known only to God," Bouwens thundered, "was to avoid the responsibility of being God's people in practice!"

But the various voices about them influenced the life of the believers' church quite deeply. The differences were so great that the conference of the brethren, which had convened at Strasbourg a year earlier, had failed to resolve them. Since then the High-German Anabaptists had espoused a more lenient course in their application of discipline. Intense persecution also led some of their members to adjust their practices of discipline, placing less emphasis on the holiness of the church. To the north, the Waterlanders likewise were less inclined to enforce the Ban on members who didn't follow a uniform practice. They taught that the church should respect the sense of the Spirit's leading in the lives of different individuals.

Jacques d'Auchy was one of the strong leaders in the

north, and a very articulate witness for the freedom of Christ. He was a salesman, who carried his products to the homes of the aristocracy and engaged them in conversation. With this means of witnessing, he had succeeded in winning numerous persons to become disciples of Christ. He and Bouwens were personal friends, although each worked in his own way. While Bouwens was concerned about getting people baptized and involved in the local churches, he respected d' Auchy highly for his success in evangelistic work. The number involved in the cause was growing and for this he was grateful.

The van den Houtes listened repeatedly to Bouwens' defense of the "pure church." They agreed with his emphasis and wanted nothing less. Without judging others, they quietly purposed to live disciplined lives, to help make their congregation a true expression of the people of God.

As the movement spread, the opposition also increased its intensity. At nearly every meeting there was a report of more persons being arrested for their faith. Many of the arrests were in the central Netherlands where the persecution was especially intense.

In late October 1557, word came that Jacques d'Auchy was arrested in Harlingen and was now held prisoner in Leeuwarden. As a gifted man, Jacques was known widely for his witness of faith. Leenaert Bouwens, knowing the details of Jacques' arrest, wrote a letter to the congregations around Ghent. Hans Timmerman, the pastor of the assembly where Willem and Soetgen attended, read the letter to the whole group.

"The councilor at Harlingen, Mr. de Wael, went out of his way to find Jacques, and invited him to his house. He treated him in a friendly manner, saying he had a special message for him. When Jacques later went to his house, Mr. de Wael welcomed him cordially and urged him to stay as his guest. He expressed great respect and love for him and a sense of indebtedness from an earlier business transaction. Jacques said he could not stay long, but promised, in response to de Wael's friendly invitation, to come again. De Wael also asked him to bring his wares, implying that he wanted to make some purchases.

"In the meantime de Wael secretly sent a messenger to Leeuwarden to the Council asking for a commissary and a bailiff. When Jacques returned, de Wael greeted him affably, sending at the same time for the bailiff. When the bailiff arrived, the traitor said: 'This is the man, apprehend him.' The bailiff thrust his neck-tongs around Jacques' neck, and demanded him to hold still while he searched him.

"Jacques cried out to de Wael in amazement, 'My lord, what have you done to betray me, when I trusted you with my life and my property? Why do you seek my life, and thirst for my blood?' But de Wael replied: 'Be calm and permit yourself to be bound. You must go with me to the prison for I have made an oath that I must fulfill.'

"After reading the cruel mandate to Jacques, he then tried to get information on four other men with an offer of leniency. But Jacques said, 'I will not betray or deceive any one. If you have anything against me, please tell me.' The traitor replied, 'I have not heard of anything you have done that is irregular, you are not apprehended on account of any crime. You are arrested because you adhere to heresy. Are you not an Anabaptist?'

"Jacques responded, 'I do not adhere to heresy, and how can I be an Anabaptist, having received but one baptism, according to the Word of the Lord, and upon my faith?'

" 'But you've left the Roman Church,' said the bailiff.

" 'Yes,' Jacques replied, 'it is not of God.'

"Now de Wael sighed deeply, his face appearing to express great sorrow. He cried out as though pained to do so, 'Oh! Jacques, now you do fall into my hands.'

"Jacques replied, 'My lord, I placed confidence in you, on account of our long-standing acquaintance, and because I had dealings with you so long. Yet I will gladly and from my heart forgive you for this. It is my earnest desire that the Lord may have mercy upon you.' De Wael thanked Jacques for his kindness, but said, 'In my opinion, I have not sinned before God, for I must act according to my oath.' Jacques said, 'Do you mean that you consider this transaction right before God and men? The time will come when you will find it otherwise.' "

The letter closed with a request that the congregation pray for Jacques, for grace to bear what he must face in the Leeuwarden prison. Timmerman asked the group to kneel in prayer. For many of them Jacques was a stranger, but for all he was their brother. They each knew that whatever happened to him affected the future of their movement.

It was early in January 1558, before Jacques had his first trial. Little news had come from the Leeuwarden prison. Earlier Jacques had prepared his confession of faith and submitted it to the magistrates for their study. He sent a copy of it to Leenaert, as his witness to the church, and now that the trial was in process his confession was being circulated in the believers' church communities. At Ghent a special meeting was called to hear his confession and to pray for his deliverance. Pastor Timmerman read the entire confession to the congregation.°

"I believe in one only God, the Father Almighty, Creator of heaven and earth, as is written, in whom Abraham, Isaac, Jacob, Moses, and all the prophets believed. Gen. 1:1; Heb. 11.

"I believe in Jesus Christ the only Son of the Father, who was from the beginning with God. And when the time which God had promised was fulfilled, this Word became flesh, and was born of the house of David, of a pure virgin espoused to a man named Joseph, of the house of David; which virgin is blessed among women. I believe that this true Son of God proclaimed the word of His Father through many signs and wonders. And after this He was delivered unto death under Pontius Pilate, and crucified and buried. I believe that this same Jesus Christ suffered for us. When we were His enemies, He suffered death for us, that those who believe in Him should not perish, but have everlasting life. I believe that this our Saviour was raised up from the dead, as He had predicted, and sits on the right hand of God His Father. John 1:14; Micah 5:2; Gal. 4:4; Rom. 1:3; Matt. 1:18; Luke 1:42; John 15:24;

°This confession is from *Martyrs Mirror*, by Thieleman J. van Braght (Scottdale: Mennonite Publishing House, 1968). Pp. 591-592. For d'Auchy's confession before the commissary and inquisitor, his martyrdom, and the fate of de Wael, see pages 592-610.

Matt. 27:2; Isa. 53:7; Rom. 5:10; John 3:16; Matt. 28:6; Mark 16:9, 19; Acts 7:56.

"I also believe in the Holy Ghost, as testified by John in his first epistle, 5th chapter, and 7th verse, where he says: 'There are three that bear record in heaven, the Father, the Word, and the Holy Ghost; and these three are one.' I also believe in the communion of the saints, whose prayer avails much. Jas. 5:16.

"I also believe in the holy church, in which are those who believe in Jesus Christ, who by one Spirit are baptized into one body, as Paul says: 'and Christ Jesus is the Head thereof, namely of the holy church, as is written.' 1 Cor. 12:13; Eph. 5:23; Col. 1:18.

"I believe that this holy church has power to open and to shut, to bind and to loose; and whatsoever they bind on earth is also bound in heaven, and whatsoever they loose on earth is also loosed in heaven. I believe that God has ordained in this holy church, apostles, prophets, teachers, bishops and deacons. Matt. 16:19; 1 Cor. 12:28.

"I also believe and confess a baptism in the name of the Father, the Son, and the Holy Ghost, even as commanded and ordained by our Lord Jesus Christ, and practiced and written of by the apostles. And I also believe that all who have received this baptism are members of the body of Jesus Christ, in the holy church. Eph. 4:5; Matt. 28:19; Acts 2:38, 41; 16:31; Rom. 6:4; Col. 2:12; 1 Cor. 12:13.

"With regard to the holy supper of Jesus Christ, I believe and confess what Christ has said concerning it, as is written: 'As they were eating the supper, Jesus took bread, and blessed it, and brake it; and gave it to the disciples, and said, Take, eat; this is my body. And he took the cup, and gave thanks, and gave it to them, saying, Drink, and divide it among yourselves; for this is my blood of the new testament, which is shed for many for the remission of sins: this do in remembrance of me.' I believe this according to the declaration of Paul, who says: 'The cup of blessing which we bless, is it not the communion of the blood of Christ? The bread which we break, is it not the communion of the body of Christ?' 'Whoso eateth my flesh, and drinketh my blood, hath eternal life; and I will raise him up at the last day.' Matt. 26:26; Luke 22:14; 1 Cor. 10:16; John 6:54.

"I confess marriage to be an ordinance of God; namely, a man and a woman united in the name of the Lord, in the holy church. 'For this cause shall a man leave father and mother, and shall cleave to his wife: and the twain shall be one flesh. Wherefore they are no more twain, but one flesh. What therefore God hath joined together, let not man put asunder. The bed is undefiled; but whoremongers and adulterers God will judge.' Gen. 2:24; 1 Cor. 7; Matt. 19:5, 6; 1 Cor. 6:16; Heb. 13:4.

"I also confess that fasting and praying is very profitable, as practiced by the apostles. Matt. 6:16; Acts 13:2.

"I regard the words of St. James as good and true, where he says: 'Confess your faults one to another, and pray one for another that ye may be healed.' Jas. 5:16. I believe that this must be done with an upright heart.

"I also confess that the higher powers are ordained of God, for the punishment of the evil, and the protection of the good; for they bear not the sword in vain; to which powers the Scriptures command us to be subject, and instruct us to pray for them, in order that, as Paul says, we may lead a quiet and peaceable life. Paul also calls the power the minister of God. Therefore since he is the minister of God, I would pray him that he would be pleased to be merciful to me, even as God is merciful. I hereby disclaim all fellowship with those who would resist the power with the sword and violence, which I regard as a doctrine of devils. Wisd. 6:3; 1 Pet. 2:13; Rom. 13:1, 4; 1 Tim. 2:2.

"I also believe in the resurrection of the dead, as it is written, that all men shall rise from the dead in their own bodies, when the Lord shall come in the clouds, with His angels; then He shall judge every one according to his

71

works. Dan. 12:2; Job 19:25; Matt. 25:31; 16:27.

"In short, I believe all that a true Christian is bound to believe of the holy church; and I believe with my whole heart in the articles of the faith, and will live and die therein. I hereby renounce all false doctrines, heresies and sects, which are not in accordance with God and His Word. And if I have erred in any respect through false doctrine, I pray the almighty God, to forgive me through His great love and mercy.

"Also, if I have sinned in any matter against the Emperor, the King, or others, I pray them to forgive me through the great love and mercy of God."

As she listened to the words of faith Soetgen was thrilled. If all their members responded to persecution in this manner, she thought, suffering would win more disciples than it discouraged!

The months dragged by slowly with no further news from Jacques. The tension was more open now and the conversations in the market became more intense, if not more free. Converts were made, friendships formed, even while arrests continued. Near the end of the year the arrests included Claesken Gaeledochter Eeuwesz, a woman who had inspired Soetgen by her faith. Soetgen had come to know her through the market where she witnessed to her freedom in Christ. She was known across Flanders and the Netherlands to the north for her influence.

Soetgen was stunned at the loss. While many Anabaptist women lived with a new freedom, Claesken's spirit had in some strange way inspired Soetgen to a sense of God's calling for herself. Converted by Gillis van Aken from the aristocratic circles of Leeuwarden, Claesken had traveled widely across their region as a spokesman for the truth. In the beginning of her work she had associated much with Elizabeth Dirks of Leeuwarden, a deaconess who worked closely with Menno. Elizabeth was one of the first deaconesses commissioned by the brotherhood, outstanding in her dedication and spirit. In fact, when she was arrested six years before in January, and drowned May 27, 1549, the bailiff thought he had arrested Menno's wife.

Following the arrest of Elizabeth and her martyrdom, Claesken spent much of her time working in the south to avoid being an easy prey to persecution where she was well known. A woman of unusual training and talent, she demonstrated the freedom and meaning of womanhood that Soetgen had long admired. She, and her husband, Hendrik, had given themselves to the spread of the gospel with all their resources. Her husband had been arrested a few weeks earlier, and now her mouth would be stopped.

A sense of destiny suddenly rolled over Soetgen. Who would counsel women in search of truth? Someone would need to take Claesken's place! What if this was her calling? What if she was to do more than witness in the local congregation? She pondered this idea long before finally sharing it with Willem.

He had been out during the day sharing his faith with men he knew in his work on the canals. Soetgen was thrilled by the way he had become an evangelist for the cause of Christ. As she watched him use his opportunities to share the gospel of grace, she yearned to be more involved herself. Now the time had come; the issue was clearly before her. They shared in this calling.

"Wim, I believe I must begin speaking for our faith. There are few women who will call others to this new life. With Claesken imprisoned, someone else will need to work as she has. I can do a similar work here in Flanders; the work must go on. It may be my lot to perpetuate her vision."

"I know," he said, his eyes dimmed with tears, "and you can do it. I've been expecting this, and I won't hold you back. But you do know what is involved, don't you, dear? Partaking of His suffering?"

His gaze met hers, deep feeling reflected in his face. Silently she nodded her head. "But faith is not unimportant. It can cost no less."

The evening meal was over and they remained at the table conversing while the children played. Willem reached to the sideboard and picked up their little glass chalice. Soetgen had brought it home from the market soon after their baptism. She had been a bit embarrassed that it was glass rather than silver, but it was all she felt they could afford. Silently he poured wine into it. Holding it to Soetgen, he said, "It is our chalice of faith, which we drink together." Her hand closed around it as she met his eyes, and held, each expressing deep feeling to the other.

Soetgen slept little during the night as she wrestled with the meaning of her conviction. By morning her mind was clear and at peace.

"Wim, I'm sure now of God's call. I must carry on the witness of personal faith which Claesken was sharing. This is my mission."

"I'm willing, Soet, to stand beside you in Christ's work — we're His disciples."

"Oh, Wim, I knew you'd say that. But I have a difficult request."

"Yes?"

"I want to go to the prison at Leeuwarden and visit Claesken. I need the satisfaction of conversation with her."

"All the way to Leeuwarden?"

"Yes, Wim, please, I must, for my own satisfaction."

A few days later Soetgen and Willem set off for the North with the old farm cart. The cow and ox plodded along slowly but steadily. It was a long trip to Friesland and the city of Leeuwarden. But she and Willem had discussed it fully. They were taking "the Way of the Vlaming," the route used by refugees from the water! She had been a young woman when the North Sea had last sent the Flemish scurrying north to their Dutch neighbors, but she remembered.

They planned to stop outside of Leeuwarden in Warga. First she would like to meet and encourage Jacques' wife before calling on Claesken. She was pregnant, and with Jacques in prison, she was going through the experience alone. Here they could learn more of events in Leeuwarden before trying to gain permission to see Claesken.

The trip was long and hard. It took more than a week to reach Warga. The wheels creaked as though complaining as they traveled mile after mile. The team plodding along slowly, kicking up dust from the tracks worn deep into the roadways. Part of the time Soetgen rested on the straw in the cart, but much of the way she sat by Willem, and they talked of the calling they now espoused.

They made careful plans for their time at Warga. Willem would do some buying for the farm while she made her visits. They would be less conspicuous in this way. Arriving in the early evening, they found lodging at an inn, and Willem took care of the animals in the stable.

The next morning she left Willem, and set out early for her call. Following directions given them, she located the house where Jacques' wife was staying. It was a row-house, and she counted the doors from the street corner. Without hesitancy she went up to the third door and knocked forcefully. To the gaze of any person on the street she appeared quite at home in Warga.

A slide was pulled back opening a small window in the door. A man's voice greeted her. "Who is calling, please?"

"Soetgen van den Houte, of near Ghent, my lord. I'm looking for the home of Peter Winands."

"I'm Peter Winands, my lady. What brings you all this distance from Ghent?"

"It's been a long trip, sir, but I'm a partner in freedom. I've come to see the wife of our brother Jacques — and hopefully Claesken."

The door flew open, and Winands said, "Quick, inside. I had no idea who you were or what could be wanted."

Soetgen stepped into the dark room. There was little light in the room, as the shutters were drawn at the windows. An oil lamp sat on a center table sputtering from the breeze. Winands shut and bolted the door, then presented Soetgen to his wife who had stood silently in the background.

"You'll pardon our care," she said, "but since we've been sheltering Jacques' wife, we've kept the front door bolted, as well as keeping the passage to the stable concealed in case we need to hide."

"Is it that bad here?" Soetgen asked.

"Indeed it is, and getting worse every day. Since Jacques was betrayed, we scarcely know who to trust. And the Anabaptist-hunters are everywhere. The bishops of Utrecht behave like little popes, dominating and taxing the country."

"But, you are keeping Jacques' wife?" Soetgen asked. "Does this not endanger you?"

"It does, true, but she is our sister and he our brother. What less would our Lord ask?" he added.

Mrs. Winands interrupted, "Sit a bit and have tea and bread. In a few minutes Estella, Jacques' wife, will be here and you can talk."

It was only a short time until Estella came into the room and Soetgen was introduced. They sat together and talked, and she heard again the details of his arrest and trial. Estella was a petite person, beautiful and quick-witted. Her French accent injected a different tone into her Dutch, giving the impression of excitement as she spoke. Her eyes shone as she spoke of her husband and of her faith.

"I went in last week to visit Jacques and they forbade me to see him. I argued and he heard my voice and called to me. I brushed by them and ran down the hall. I'm heavy with child and the guards didn't catch hold of me.

"I found him there, as he reached his hands through

the bars. We embraced for a moment, the rough bars between us."

Soetgen listened as the tears ran down Estella's face, her own eyes filling as well.

"Oh, my Jacques, he was beaten and bruised. . . . They've handled him so cruelly. Even his leather clothes are bloody and torn from their torture. I tried to comfort him, but the guards caught me and pulled us apart."

"How dreadful," Soetgen cried. "They wouldn't even let you talk?"

"No, scarcely for a moment. Jacques pleaded with them, asking them to leave his lamb with him, but they dragged me away, those soul-murderers, enemies of the cross of Christ!"

Here Estella dropped her face into her hands and sobbed. Soetgen placed her hand on Estella's shoulder. "We can only pray and trust God to show the strength of His truth even in suffering."

Soetgen spent the day sharing with Estella, enjoying her spirit and faith. They walked through the city and found a bench under the lime trees along the canal. They watched dead leaves drop from the trees to be carried away by the flow of the water. They talked, and she learned more about Estella, and about the suffering in Leeuwarden.

"I'm most grateful, Soetgen, for these past few years especially, that Jacques and I have had together. Since we've known Christ our love has been so wonderful."

Her eyes were bright and her face aglow as she spoke. "I know what you mean. It has been the same

78

for us," Soetgen added, then stopped as she waited for Estella to say more.

"This is the wonderful thing about our movement — women have found a new sense of freedom and responsibility in Christ."

She continued, "If there is one thing the Inquisition can't handle it's this new freedom among Christian women. This will not be crushed no matter how hard they try."

Soetgen reviewed her plans to visit Claesken, if she was admitted. It was early evening and time to rejoin Willem. Before leaving she joined them in prayer for those in prison and asked God to open the door for a talk with Claesken. With a promise to stop by in the morning before leaving for Leeuwarden, she was off to find Willem.

In the early morning Soetgen had joined the Winands and they had just finished eating together when there was a sharp knock on the door. They all sat quietly for a moment. The knock sounded again, with more urgency. Mr. Winands arose and went to the door, opened the little window to look out, then slowly pulled back the bolt, and opened the door. On the steps stood a man holding a scroll in his hand.

"Here," he said breathlessly, thrusting it into the hands of Mr. Winands. "You should have this. It's from Jacques. He left it in his cell. He's dead."

"Dead!" Estella cried. "No!"

"I'm sorry, ma'am, but it's true, he's gone."

Soetgen slipped over to sit beside Estella, placing an arm around her in comfort. Mr. Winands pulled the guard inside and closed the door.

"Tell us more," he said. "We'd like to know."

The man hesitated, looking at Jacques' wife. At his pause, she lifted her face, wet with tears, "Please do; we want to know."

"There is little I can share," he began. "He was found dead in his cell this morning, lying in his own blood. Someone entered his cell while he slept and stabbed him." He paused again, looking at Estella who wept silently.

"He was a brave man. Many of us were impressed by him. That's why I'm here. I can't say I believe as he did, but at least I can say his belief worked for him. I had come to love that man. There's quite a stir around the prison this morning. We didn't expect him to be killed like this. It's awful."

The man stopped, looked about at each, then at Estella. "He told me where you were and wanted you to have this, his last words." He turned, pulled the bolt, and stepped out the door.

Mr. Winands stepped over to Estella's side, knelt beside her, and began to pray. "Heavenly Father, we thank Thee for the joy of Thy salvation, the assurance that Jacques belonged to Thee, and is with Thee. Come by Thy Holy Spirit and strengthen Estella for this cross she must bear. Use this event to magnify the meaning of true faith. Even through this death we pray that the gospel will be spread. Through Christ our Lord. Amen."

Estella's voice joined the others as they all said, "Amen."

80

7 The prison was dark and foreboding as Soetgen stood before it. This was the goal of her trip, to see Claesken, to discover whether her sense of calling was a genuine down-to-earth calling or a romantic notion. The past few days had been quite traumatic — the burial of the broken body of Jacques, the reaction of the community to his having been murdered, and her inner concerns about coming to the prison to call on Claesken. It was enough to shake anyone's faith in the cause, but the conviction was still within her. She had prayed and asked God to go before her. She hoped that with so much community reaction over Jacques' death the guards would be more lenient about visits.

Taking a deep breath, Soetgen crossed the cobblestone street and stood before the guard at the door. He was a large man with a broad blond moustache.

"Sir, I have come from Ghent to call on an acquaintance who is here in prison."

"Yes," he inquired, "and who might that be? A runaway husband?" And he laughed harshly.

"No, this is not so personal a matter. Her name is Claesken, a friend I met in the market."

"The psalm-singing heretic," he interrupted. "And what might you want with her?"

"To bring her greetings from friends, to talk with her about why she is here, and I'd like to give her this," she added, gesturing to the basket on her arm.

He looked at it with interest. Quickly she pulled back the cloth exposing freshly baked rolls. "Help yourself, sir, I believe there are enough."

Reaching into the basket, he lifted two, and stood eating in silence as he continued looking at her. Her eyes never wavered, and finally he dropped his. "All right," he said, "you may go in, but only for a few minutes or we'll keep you. Upstairs, to the right and back to the end of the hall."

Soetgen stepped inside, her heart pounding. She walked slowly back the dark hall, past cells from which voices called out to her. Climbing the stairs, she started back the narrow passage, her eyes adjusting themselves to the darkness. The hall ended at a heavy door. It had a small opening covered with a metal grill. Placing her face against it, she peered into the cell. The room was small and dark. A stench hit Soetgen's nostrils from refuse which had accumulated on the floor.

In the middle of the room was a log, designed to stretch a woman prisoner during torture. It was empty. Her eyes moved to the far corner, and then she saw her. A narrow aperture in the wall permitted light and air to move into that corner of the room. The woman sitting there gazed back at her with an open, friendly expression.

"Claesken," she whispered.

"Yes." The voice was calm. "And who are you?"

"I'm Soetgen van den Houte, from Ghent, your sister in Christ. I've come to talk with you, to share your ministry."

"My ministry seems to be one of suffering," she replied. Getting up slowly, she walked toward the door. Silently she stood looking into Soetgen's eyes, a smile of recognition crossed her face. "My sister in Christ," she breathed, "may He keep His hand upon you. Ours is not an easy lot, breaking the shackles of a fallen church and seeing His church come again. You do know His freedom, don't you?"

Soetgen nodded, her eyes filling with tears as she saw the marks of torture on the woman who stood before her. "I do, that's why I'm here. My husband and I were baptized by Leenaert Bouwens. We are witnesses for Christ in our area."

"Tell me," Claesken said, "how things are going outside. I know of Jacques' death. I didn't hear him singing anymore, and then yesterday in torture the bailiff threatened me with a sudden death like Jacques met! But what is happening beyond?"

"The movement continues to grow," Soetgen replied. "In fact, among the populace there are more with us than against us. Even many not of our faith are quite sympathetic. The cause won't die, even if some of us must." Here she stopped, embarrassed that she had said this to Claesken, in prison.

"It's all right," she answered. "We knew this might come when we accepted His baptism."

For nearly half an hour Claesken shared her faith and vision. She encouraged Soetgen to minister to the women, introducing them to the freedom of Christ. "Help them discover that they are persons who also need a faith in Christ. This is your call, Soetgen, to be a counselor of women, a witness to the dignity and grace of Christian womanhood."

The sound of voices, then of steps on the stairs arrested their conversation. Claesken said, "Here, quick, take this letter and get it to my family."

She pressed a scroll through the bars and Soetgen quickly hid it under her mantle. "You may read it," Claesken said, "but please get it to my family afterward; it may be my last will and testament."

The guards were approaching now and Soetgen knew she would have to leave. She had forgotten her basket until the moment. Quickly she pressed several fresh rolls through the grillwork into Claesken's hands. Claesken lifted one, broke off a piece, broke it again and pressed a piece through the bars: "His body, which was broken for us," she said and began eating hers. Soetgen placed the piece in her mouth as their eyes met.

A hand closed on her shoulder. "Time's up, or do you want us to lock you up as well?" Soetgen turned and began walking back the hall. Turning at the steps, she looked back at the face peering out through the grill.

"Farewell, Claesken, farewell."

"Farewell, Soetgen . . . until then," and Claesken's voice was lost in the orders of the guards.

Out on the street Soetgen breathed deeply. She was free to go, and yet those brief moments had bound her in a strange way to the woman in the cell. She felt almost as if she had left a part of herself behind. The simple, brief act of sharing the Lord's Supper through prison bars was etched indelibly in her mind. Walking down the street, she reached beneath her mantle and clutched the scroll. The road stretched before her to Warga and the inn where she and Willem had agreed to meet. As she walked, she hastened her step. It was Willem and home to the children that she was interested in now, and the journey was long. Several weeks with their uncle and aunt caring for them was not too long, but she was anxious to see them.

The wind beat against her and she dropped her head as she moved into it. Overhead the gulls wheeled and circled, screaming into the gale. She stopped to rest. Nature is free, she thought, as she watched a sea gull swinging on motionless wings in the strong air. Its beauty stirred her emotions, and tears filled her eyes. "Would that Claesken were free," she thought, "and yet, wasn't she, in spirit?"

By eventide she was back at the inn and found Willem sitting alone at a table.

"My darling," she said, "how wonderful to be together."

"And good it is, my lamb," he replied. "I've missed you so very much. I'm not much for this Frisian cooking, you know," he added mischievously.

"Is that all you've missed?" she asked, with a bit of a twinkle in her eyes.

"No, my darling, I missed you."

"And I missed you, Wim. I love you more every day, and even more so since I love you in Christ."

"Did you see Claesken, Soet? Did you get into the prison?"

"I did, Wim, and I'm so glad we came. But I'll carry the memory of her words and the sight of her in that cell as long as I live."

He looked at her thoughtfully, then said, "You're tired now; you can tell me the details tomorrow after you have rested."

"But what of Claesken's confession? I have a single copy, Wim. What shall I do with it?"

"Take it along; you can copy it to be sure it doesn't get destroyed, and send it to Workum."

He had arranged for a room where they would lodge for the night, and early morning saw them on their way. As the cart creaked and jostled along the road, Soetgen told Willem the details of her visit with the Winands and of her visit with Claesken. He reached over and clasped her hand in his as they rode for some time in silence. There was a sense of destiny in the mind of each as they pondered these events.

They secured lodging at an inn that night, for five thalers, and slept the sleep of the weary. At early dawn they were on their way. As the miles passed, they enjoyed the time together, watching the gulls, laughing together about little notes of interest, remarking about the beauty of their homeland — its soft colors, gray and green, of sand dunes, of marsh and meadow. They were anxious now to be at home.

The last miles dragged wearily by, but at last they were on familiar ground. She scarcely noticed the willows swaying in the breeze, the song of the soaring lark, the lazy sweep of the windmill arms, or the sunlight glittering on the distant lakes. She saw their cottage in the distance. The children were at the gate, and then running across the field. She took them in her arms and whispered endearments.

The children were overjoyed to see them, wanting

to hear everything about the trip. As she told of Jacques' death, she suddenly noticed how they were absorbing every detail. She cut the story short, and turned the conversation to other things.

Later they shared in family prayers, and then sent the children off to bed. Picking up the roll of paper Claesken had given her, she opened it and began to read as Willem listened:[*]

The Account of My Trials of Faith. First of all the commissary interrogated me concerning my name, the place I was from, my age, and other like things. He then asked me: "Are you baptized?" to which I answered, "Yes." He asked, "Who baptized you?" and I replied, "Jelis of Aix-la-Chapelle."

His face flushed in anger, and he spat out, "That deceiver; he himself has renounced his belief. How did he do when he baptized you?" "He baptized me in the name of the Father, the Son, and the Holy Ghost."

He then asked, "Where did you receive baptism?" And I told him, "At Workum in the field." Next he wanted to know, "Were there others present?" When I said, "Yes," he asked, "Who are they?" I responded, "I have forgotten." To his next question, "What brought you there?" I again said, "I have forgotten." I could truthfully give this answer both times.

He asked me, "Why don't Anabaptist women stay at home and be subject to their husbands?" I answered, "Women are subject to their husbands in Christ." He replied, "But you travel the country to stir up other women to disregard their family duties." I explained, "Women make better wives and mothers when they are free in Christ."

After some moments he tried a new approach. "Are

[*]For a complete account of the confessions of Claesken see *Martyrs Mirror*, pp. 611-616.

87

your children not baptized?" and I told him, "My youngest two are not." He asked me, "Why did you not have your children baptized?" And I said, "Because I was satisfied with them as the Lord had given them to me." He responded, "Why were you so satisfied with Abraham and Sicke, and not with Douwe; you had Douwe baptized?" I explained, "I did not know it then." He quickly asked, "What did you not know then?" I didn't give him words to quote, and said simply, "What I know now!" But he continued, "What do you know now?" And when I answered, "What the Lord has given me to know," he pressed again, "What has the Lord given you to know?" I replied, "I cannot find it in the Scriptures, that this ought to be." He wanted to know, "How long have you not been to church?" And I told him, "Not for nine or ten years."

These are the questions which he put to me; but he used far more words. When I did not readily answer him, he said that I had a dumb devil in me, that the devil transformed himself into an angel of light in us, and that we were all heretics. He then read to me the articles I had confessed, and said it should come before the lords, and that if I desired it, he would write it differently. I replied, "You need not change anything."

There was much more to the letter, but Soetgen stopped reading. Her brow was wrinkled in thought, her mind back at Leeuwarden in the prison cell. She could see Claesken's face at the bars of the door, hear her words, "His body, which was broken for us," and even taste the bread in her thoughts.

"Wim, I talked with her nearly half an hour before the guards asked me to leave. I can't copy Claesken's role, but I share her vision. In some way I must continue her ministry. Somehow I believe women may listen to a woman with perception."

"It's all right, Soet, if you feel God calling you to this, but couldn't you serve in our community so that our little ones wouldn't be without your care?"

"Oh, of course, Wim, there is more than I can get done among the thousands around Ghent, and our little lambs will not lose their mother."

Willem smiled and pressed her hand in his. "There is no power that a woman has that is greater than the freedom to shape her own home and its influence in the community."

"Thank you, Wim, you make me feel more important than I really am. There is no cause for me that isn't enhanced by my being your wife."

It was very dark in the old house, and Soetgen lay in Willem's arms. Theirs was a love of deep contentment in each other. Their joy at being together again made them wholly each other's. They had shared tonight the rapture of the early days of their marriage, but to the ecstasy of body was now added the ecstasy of mind and spirit.

Long into the night she lay in thought while he slept. Their new faith did not rob them of lovers' bliss, she thought, it made it more complete. Stretching herself sleepily beside Willem, she wished that somehow this joy would never end.

8 In protecting their faith men tend to become defensive. Because of this human trait, all was not well in the Anabaptist movement. An association was begun between the congregations of Harlingen, Franeker, Leeuwarden, and Dokkum to the north, forming a common discipline. A cleavage between the Waterlanders and the followers of Menno became more and more apparent. Cultural and temperamental differences between the Frisians and the Old Flemish who had migrated from the south created deep tensions. The Frisians accused the Flemish of being worldly in their way of dress, and the Flemish accused the Frisians of being worldly in their homes. The Waterlanders referred to themselves as Doopsgezinden, while the followers of Menno were becoming known as Mennisten. However, many of the preachers opposed the name, saying "We do not call ourselves by Menno but by Christ." The van den Houtes, living in a trade community in the southern part of the Netherlands, were being influenced by both parties. Their past experiences with Menno and Leenaert had led them to respect the more rigid group very highly. With increased persecution, they were sympathetic to those who wanted the discipline to be less rigid.

With the confusion caused by these differences Soetgen and Willem were busy seeking to encourage the house churches in their region. She especially became a familiar figure, walking the roads, calling on home after home to share her faith with other women.

It was midsummer and the flax was ripe. Its golden color spread across the land, and the neighbors were all busy. Yet amidst the activity of exchanging help in the fields this was a good time for conversation. Work and witness could be tied together. The spread of faith was continuous and not easily detected.

Her brother and sisters were a special concern to Soetgen. Nettie and Hendrik were interested in the movement but were as yet uncommitted. She was especially concerned for her sister, Betken. Earlier Betken had urged her to investigate the believers' church and now she held back herself. In fact, she lived in fear for Soetgen's life and constantly warned her that her activity would come to the attention of the bailiff or the burgomaster. But Soetgen's only answer was, "Show me a better way with the Word of the gospel and I will renounce mine!"

Instead of being intimidated by Betken's warning, she sought to win her sister to a commitment of faith.

"I just can't, Soetgen," she said, when they were last together, "at least not without my husband. You know that."

"But if you commit yourself to the way of Christ, you can help him."

"I'm not so sure. He might just resent it. I belong to him, you know."

"Yes, I know. You can decide for yourself. Faith is a personal matter."

But Betken had only shook her head no. She was a

follower, she said, one who would always follow the one dearest her. They would have to win her husband.

Nearly six months had now passed since Soetgen had visited the prison at Leeuwarden. Her thoughts and prayers had often turned to Claesken in prison. And then without warning the word came of her martyrdom. She had finally been tried, sentenced, and burned at the stake! Soetgen was in Ghent when she heard the news. The journey home seemed twice as long. She had known it was only a matter of time; yet she walked as in a daze. There was no limit to the opposition to the movement; that was clear.

That night, she and Willem sat late talking of the course they had chosen. He held her hands in his across the table. The candle flickered between them. It was time to retire, but Willem reached to the sideboard and picked up the little chalice. He held it in his hands between them, turning it slowly as they watched the figures on its sides. "Our chalice, dearest, our chalice of faith."

She took it and lifted it to her lips; their eyes met above it. She drank and handed it to him, watching as he lifted it, watching him swallow, and gaze at her as she responded. "Our chalice, though it be for some a chalice of blood."

The number of arrests in their area now became frightening. People whom they had known close at hand were arrested and summarily slain. The act that shook the community to its very heart was the arrest and beheading of five brothers! The story of the barbarous deed spread across the area with the news of their noble spirit in death. The youngest had asked to go first, lest watching the others he weaken and recant. Each in turn had then laid his head on the block without a struggle. The populace was stirred with helpless indignation. A cloud of gloom settled across the country.

The van den Houtes did not talk of this before the children. But that same evening they gathered them around before dinner and talked to them of what to do should their parents be taken away. It was all Soetgen could do to keep back the tears as she watched Tanneken's face and looked into Bet's large round eyes. David alone seemed to understand.

"You mean they might take you to prison because of our church?" he asked.

"Yes, because of our belief," she responded. "Not everyone believes as your father and I. We are followers only of Christ, you understand, not of men. We know no superior save Christ."

David nodded his head. "You mean we aren't going to obey anyone but God."

"Yes, son, that's what we mean, to obey only God and His Word. If anything should happen to us, son, we want you to take your sisters and get someone to take you to Aunt Nettie and Uncle Hendrik. They'll look out for you. Promise me?"

"I promise," David said.

"We'll go, Mother," little Betken replied.

"Promise," whispered little Tanneken.

Soetgen got up and went to the cupboard. Her back to the children, she lifted her apron to wipe her eyes. Willem sat silently, looking at each of the children. "You'll remember, David, yet we pray it won't happen."

David nodded with a wisdom beyond his years. Soetgen soon had the table set, and as they ate, it was as though the conversation had not happened — yet each remembered. The children were exceptionally thoughtful of each other throughout the evening. At evening prayers each prayed in turn and asked God to keep and protect them.

The next days passed with scarcely a word about the conversation. Their work kept them busy. The children helped in the field and with the cheese. While they worked she explained to them what she and their father were doing the many times that one of them was away sharing their faith. At evening Soetgen read to them from the Scripture, and she and Willem together taught them what the passages meant. Then, one afternoon, Willem came hurrying home from Ghent. He found Soetgen and the children at the barn milking. She knew at once that something was wrong by the grave expression on his face.

"I'm afraid the time has come, Soetgen. A troop of infantry is in Ghent making arrests. They have a list of names and are asking about each person. Our name was heard as they inquired."

Soetgen's hand went to her throat. "Our name, Wim?"

"Yes, ours, my lamb. When I heard, I set out across the fields to reach you first."

"Come here, children," she called. "Leave your work, at once, we must talk to you."

They came quickly and Willem began. "Children,

95

this is the time we told you about. The soldiers are coming. They may take us away."

The two girls began to cry and threw themselves into Soetgen's arms. David stood against his father and Willem placed his arm about him. Great tears rolled down his cheeks even as he stood with head erect.

"You must stay here in the barn where we hide you until you are sure the soldiers are gone." Soetgen began. "Later you can go to Timmermans and ask to stay there tonight — tomorrow they'll help you on your way to your aunt's and uncle's." She looked at Willem, and he nodded his agreement.

"We'll trust God to take care of you little ones. Don't ever forget why we are taken away from you, and what we have taught you. Each of you must be followers of Christ too. This suffering will pass and the world will recognize the truth. By the time you are our age, there will be freedom for you to live your faith."

Soetgen and Willem each embraced the children and held them long. They hid them, then, back of the feedbox, and covered the place with hay. The children heard their parents pray over them, whisper good-bye, and listened to their steps as they left the barn.

Just as they reached the gate by the house, they saw dust in the distance, and then the figures of mounted men riding toward them. They stood and waited, hand in hand, their hearts pounding as the horsemen drew near.

The leader jerked his horse to a stop before them,

a spray of earth touching them lightly.

"The van den Houtes?" he asked.

"We are," Willem's voice was calm.

"You are now the prisoners of his majesty the king. You will come with us."

One of the commissaries had swung down and approached them with a rope.

"Need you bind us?" Willem asked. "We can follow better if you permit us to walk free."

The commissary looked at his superior officer. His brow creased with wrinkles as he reflected a moment, then said, "We'll try it, but if there is any trouble, we'll tie you like a dog, and if necessary drag you."

With this he turned his horse, and they fell in behind, walking toward Ghent. The others brought up the rear.

As they trudged down the road, the horses kicked up dust in their faces. Several times they glanced back at their little cottage, and at the barn where the children were hid, their view obscured by the horsemen following. At least there was no fire, and they were relieved.

Willem took Soetgen's hand as they walked along. At the pace they were made to walk there was little breath for conversation. It was quiet, except for the regular sound of the horses hooves on the road, and the sound of their heavy breathing. The way was familiar, for they had walked it often to and from market. Today, however, they felt like strangers in their own land.

At several points other horsemen joined the group, bringing with them prisoners they had gathered.

Soetgen and Willem knew them all, for not only were they neighbors but they were brothers and sisters in the faith. They had often met together to worship and to exhort one another.

By the time they reached Ghent and the prison, it was late evening. Soetgen shuddered as they were brought to it. Willem took her hand and squeezed it. "The cup which He gives. . . ."

Gratefully she smiled at him. "We may not get to see each other more," he added, "and I'm not as free with words as some to defend my case. Whatever you hear, Soetgen, my lamb, you can be sure that at least I will have kept the faith."

"I know, Wim, and I believe you. Let's pray for each other."

The group was being herded toward the prison while they talked. Suddenly the commissaries ordered the group to stop. The bailiff lifted his hand for silence. "We've made these arrests and brought you here because of your subversive action. You are a threat to our country by your rejection of the altar and the Church."

He paused and looked around at the group in silence, then continued. "But we've decided to be lenient. We're going to keep you men, and with this as a warning we'll let the women go. You women may go home where you belong and keep quiet."

The group was stunned into immobility. Then there was a stir, and the couples were in each other's arms. They knew this would doubtless be their last time together. But this was only for a moment, for the commissaries quickly moved among them, ordering

98

the women to move out, and leading the men into cells.

Soetgen stood in silence, scalding tears running down her face, as she watched Willem led away. At the door he looked back, their eyes meeting, and then he was gone. She turned and stumbled blindly down the street. She was free to go home, and yet it was as though she were bound, for her heart was with Willem.

She felt a hand on her arm, and looking up she saw that it was a distant neighbor, Martha van Leuven. "May I walk along," Martha asked, "and keep you company?"

"Of course," Soetgen responded. "I need it right now, and we're better off together."

"I need it too," Martha said. "The comfort of another's faith helps my own."

They walked in silence for a while. Their faces were flushed and their eyes were bright from the excitement. They paused to rest and began talking about their husbands, about how they would react under pressure. Soetgen was sure Willem would stand by his faith, even though he might not so ably express his defense.

As they hurried on, Soetgen scarcely noticed the familiar landscape through the numbing mist of shock that encompassed her. The evening sky was red as the sun dropped below the horizon. Suddenly they came to the fork of the road that led Soetgen one way and Martha in the other direction toward Antwerp. Her thoughts were suddenly of the children. "I must hurry, Martha. We left the children in the barn, and told them to go to the Timmermans and later to their uncle's and aunt's. I wonder where they are?" A note of fear crept into her voice for the first time.

"And if they went to Timmerman's, where would that be?"

"Several miles across the fields to the northwest.

"That would be in my direction, then?"

"Yes, I suppose."

"Then I'll go with you, and help you find them."

"Would you?" There was evident relief in Soetgen's voice. "It would be nice to have your company."

They hurried along the road, stumbling a bit in their haste, as they slipped into the deep cart tracks. It was quite dark by the time they arrived at the house. Soetgen said, "I'll get a lantern and we'll check the barn before going on. We'll need a light anyway."

Hurrying to the barn, she led the way to the feed-box. "The hay," Soetgen exclaimed, "it hasn't been moved!"

Quickly she pulled it back, lifted the wooden lid while Martha held the lantern. She stopped and tears ran down her face. There they lay, sound asleep, little Betken and Tanneken in each other's arms, and David curled up next to them. There were streaks on his cheeks from his tears.

"God bless them," she breathed, "and keep them in His hand," she added, "always."

9 The next morning Soetgen was up early, preparing for the day. Martha had helped her bring the children to the house and had spent the night with them. The girls had only half-awakened as they carried them in. But David had come wide-awake at once when she touched him, had thrown his arms around her and wept. Late into the night she heard little noises from his bed that told her he was not asleep. She had lain awake, herself listening to the soft moans of the wind, as though it shared their sadness.

It all seemed like a bad dream this morning, except that Willem was gone. She remembered so vividly his expression as he walked into the prison. Now she would need to help the children understand. After breakfast she talked long with them about their faith, about why their father was in prison, and about the opposition to the true church of Christ. Martha sat and listened, looking out into the distance. Her thoughts were with her own husband and his lot, even while she listened to Soetgen teaching the children from the Bible.

Soetgen was wearing a long cloak over her plain gown, her hair was swept back in wavy bands tucked under her cap, and her face was serene, though lined by the cares of the last hours. Her voice was mellow but strong as she spoke to the children.

"My little ones, it is hard for you to understand all that this means, since you are so young. But the time will come for you to fill your role in our Father's kingdom. You must seek to know and follow God's will."

"But how can we know God's will, Mother, without you and Father to guide us?" Betken asked.

"By studying the Bible, Bet, and obeying it. In the first book in the Bible we read of men who are examples for us. We are not to be like Esau who gave up his father's blessing for a mess of pottage. But his brother Jacob lived by faith that his father's blessing was important."

"Do you mean that for us to seek God's blessing is the same as for Jacob?" David queried.

"Yes, David. You must read the Bible and try to understand what it says so that you know how to decide the right and true way. You can choose life or death, good or evil — it is up to you."

Soetgen paused as she mentioned the choice between life and death, her mind going to Willem in prison. Better to die physically, she thought, than to be dead while living.

"Children, there is a way of life that is evil, that only shares the dying things of the world. These are things you cannot do, David, without losing your dignity as a man of God. I am talking about evil practices such as lying, cheating, gambling, envy, hatred, drunkenness, covetousness, filthy conversation, dancing, and immoral conduct. Many people of the world call these only amusements, but God calls them sins. Peter writes about this in the fourth chapter of his first book."

"Don't most people live like you and Father?" Betken asked.

"No, darling, they don't. Most of the people in the world don't walk with God. There is more earth to make earthen vessels than gold to make golden ones. Jesus said, 'Many are called but few are chosen ones.' Many do not obey their call. In John's Gospel we read that Jesus said, 'My sheep hear my voice, and they follow me.' You must follow Christ even though you suffer from the many who are against Him."

Soetgen turned in her Bible to Matthew the eleventh chapter and read verse twelve: " 'The kingdom of heaven suffereth violence and the violent take it by force.' You must count the kingdom of heaven so important that in spite of suffering you are diligent to be faithful. The Bible also says, 'Ye must through much tribulation enter into it.' "

"This kingdom, Mother, is it heaven?" David's voice was earnest as he spoke.

"Yes, finally, but it begins now. It is like belonging to the Netherlands even though the Spanish now rule us. We belong to God even though the forces of evil rule in the world. But His kingdom will come."

She paged in the Bible to the Gospel of John and read verse thirty-three of chapter sixteen: " 'In the world ye shall have tribulation, but be of good cheer, I have overcome the world.' " Then she turned to Revelation, chapter two, and read verse ten, " 'Ye shall have tribulation for a little while, but be of good cheer and be faithful unto death, and I will give you a crown of life.' And again, in chapter nineteen we read, 'The marriage of the Lamb is come, and his

103

E.B.Wallase

wife hath made herself ready. And to her was granted that she should be arrayed in fine linen, clean and white; for the fine linen is the righteousness of the saints. Blessed are they which are called unto the marriage supper of the Lamb.' You see, children," Soetgen added, "God has made us heirs in Christ of all the riches of heaven."

"I sure wish," David broke in, "that I knew the Bible like you do."

"You will," Soetgen said, "the more you read it."

Soetgen closed the Bible, smiled at the children, "That is enough for this morning. Run along to your work — and play." Quietly they slipped out of the house and off to the barn together.

Later in the morning Soetgen was alone. The old house creaked in the force of the wind as it blew unchecked across the polders. She picked up the little glass chalice and stood gazing into it, recalling the experiences of faith she and Willem shared. Her thoughts were of Ghent, of Willem in the prison, suffering the indignities and harassment of his captors. The chalice faded in the blank stare of her tear-filled eyes. His face swam into view and then was gone. The wind whistled by the eaves with a haunting note. In this daze her hand began to relax and the chalice dropped with a crash at her feet, spraying the floor with glass.

Startled, her hand went to her throat — their chalice was broken! Did this have meaning? Was their sharing over? Was the fellowship of their chalice past? She stood looking at the broken chalice at her feet. Suddenly she remembered the words of the Master, "I will not drink again of this cup until I drink it new with you in the kingdom of my Father." That will be true for us, she said to herself. It's not over. We will share it in all eternity! A smile lighted her face, the darkness was past. Quickly she swept up the glass. Fresh courage came to strengthen her. She went back to her tasks with a new composure.

Through the day several friends of the neighborhood stopped briefly to express their concern and promise to pray for Willem. Martha left at noon to make her way to her home. Toward evening Nettie and Hendrik came. Hendrik helped David take care of the chores at the barn while Nettie took over at the house.

"Sit a while, Soetgen, and let me prepare the evening meal."

"Thank you, Nettie, not that I'm so tired, but it's a comfort to have you here."

"We decided to come as soon as we heard. We didn't know until today. What if they had kept you? What of the children?"

"Wim and I hid them in the barn when we knew the soldiers were coming. We told them to stay there until it was safe, then to come to you."

Nettie smiled and said in a hushed voice, "Thank you for trusting us. I hope nothing further happens, but if it should, you can count on us."

"It may, Nettie. I don't intend to sit silently by while all this is happening."

"What do you mean to do?"

"I plan to be a Bible teacher like Claesken, to minister to women, to help them discover the new life in Christ."

Nettie's hand went to her throat. "But — but that is dangerous; you'll be arrested too."

"It may be, Nettie, but this is God's call for me. The revolution of life isn't finished. I'm tired of seeing people miss knowing Christ because of the empty forms and tyrannical treatment of the priests."

"Oh, Soetgen, I respect your faith; you are so sure, but must we oppose the powers?"

"It is not we who oppose, but they. Let them give us freedom to walk with Christ, freedom to be real men and women, and they and our country will be the better for it. Let them oppose this freedom and they themselves will be enslaved by their tyranny."

The fire of conviction burned in Soetgen. Nettie stood looking at her in amazement. Willem's imprisonment had made her more determined; it hadn't dissuaded her. Suddenly the two sisters were weeping in each other's arms. Nettie said, "I understand, Soetgen, and you must be true — there are many who need you. We admire you even if we don't agree."

After the evening meal Nettie and Hendrik left. The dishes and pans were washed, and Soetgen gathered the children for an evening Bible study. She would help others as she could, but not to the neglect of her own. Should she be taken away, they must be prepared. And so again she taught them.

"This evening, children, I want to admonish you to attain a character above reproach. Beware of lying, for the Scripture teaches, 'Liars have no part in the kingdom of God,' and again, 'Lying lips are an abomination to the Lord.' Beware of lying, for he that deals in lies is loved by no one. Guard your tongue to speak no evil. Never practice deceit nor be guilty of backbiting. Paul teaches us in Romans to live peacefully with all men if it be possible."

"But how can we live at peace with all," David asked, "when they persecute us?"

"The Bible says 'as much as lies within you,' David. That means that you are to do your part. Obey your parents, and anyone whose bread you eat or who admonishes you to virtue. Always be diligent to do your work, wherever you are. Paul says that if any will not work, neither shall he eat. The Bible also says, 'Be diligent to labor that you may have to give to him that needeth.' Never turn your face away from the poor. 'Whoso stoppeth his ears at the cry of the poor, he also shall cry himself, but shall not be heard.' Son, if you have abundance, give alms accordingly: if you have but little; do not be afraid to give according to that little."

"I hope that I too can help others," David said.

"Me, too," Betken added.

"It is your spirit that counts, children," Soetgen smiled. "Be diligent in prayer, and love the poor, for Christ also was poor for our sakes. Paul writes, 'Be merciful even as your heavenly Father is merciful, for such shall be blessed, and shall obtain mercy.' Learn to be meek and lowly in heart, for Jesus said such shall inherit the earth. Also He taught us, 'Blessed are the pure in heart, for they shall see God!' "

"What does He mean, Mother, by pure in heart?" little Tanneken whispered.

"My dear, He means let no impure thoughts remain in your hearts or minds. If you will sing and think about psalms, hymns, and spiritual songs, evil thoughts will have no room.

"And now one more Scripture before bed, from the words of Jesus. He taught us to avoid being proud. Wherever you go, think of yourselves as the least; do not think you know more than others. Always permit yourselves to be taught in the Scripture by those who are above you, and always be silent when others speak. Jesus said in Matthew twenty-three, verse fourteen, 'Humble yourself before all men; for whosoever shall exalt himself shall be abased; but he that shall humble himself shall be exalted.' Christ, who is the greatest, made Himself the least, for an example unto us."

Soetgen closed the Bible, and they bowed their heads to pray. She prayed for each of them and for their father in prison. When she finished, each one kissed her good night and climbed into bed.

When the children were off to bed, all was quiet in the little cottage. Soetgen sat alone with her thoughts, praying for Willem, longing for him. If only she would get some word from him.

Several days later Soetgen left the children with Nettie and set off for Ghent. She had little to take to market, but with butter and buttermilk she had a good reason for her trip should she be asked. It was news of Willem that she wanted, but she could sell what she had at the market. The children continually asked about their father, and she could only reply, "We must pray and trust our Lord to take care of him."

Scarcely feeling the weight of her basket, she hastened along the road. Nearing the city she joined others en route to the market. As they passed along the river Lys, she scarcely noticed its calm face or the ornate houses that stretched along its banks.

At the market she found Martha van Leuven and other women whose men had been arrested. No one had any satisfying information. All that could be learned was that the men were in separate cells, being interrogated and held for trial as heretics.

Soetgen used the opportunity to cultivate acquaintances and asked various women to plan meetings in their homes for the sharing of faith. By late afternoon she had arranged one for each day of the week following. As she started for home, she chose the streets that led her past the prison. Beyond the old frame wool mill she stopped, and looked at the impregnable walled structure at the end of the street.

From where she stood its walls looked cold and sullen. Willem was somewhere inside, locked in a dungeon. Her heart cried out to him, and she shuddered as she prayed, "Dear Lord, make him strong. Keep him in his hour of trial."

She turned and made her way across town to the road toward home. She passed the city hall with its impressive moorish front. She gazed up at the great belfry where for three centuries the large dragon sent by Emperor Boudewijn of Flanders from Constantinople breathed out its symbol of terror. She shuddered as she thought of the horrors of misdirected power. How long, she asked in her mind, will men fight God and rob their fellowmen of the freedom to be God's men? She looked back at the city hall, and cried out in her heart, "Your eighty thousand fighting men are not

110

enough to stop the march of truth — men and women alike will yet be free, by God's grace!"

The way seemed extra long. While going back to the children, she was leaving Willem bound in Ghent. More than once she stumbled from the tears in her eyes rather than from ruts in the road. The children were excited when they saw her coming. The questions tumbled over each other. "Did you get to see Father?" "When is he coming home?" "How are they treating Father?" This last from David.

"No, my dear ones, I couldn't see him. He's in the prison. No one may talk with the prisoners."

"How long will he be there, Mother?" Tanneken asked.

"None of us know. One of these days they will have a trial. They will have him appear before a group of men, and he will tell them what he believes."

"Then they'll let him go," little Betken said, "when they find out he's a good man."

Soetgen drew Betken to her lap. "I hope so, my little one. He is a good man, we know that."

After they had eaten, Soetgen called them around her. "Children, we're being used of the Lord to help bring His kingdom. This means suffering, like Father is doing now, and it might even mean that some of us will have to die. But it will be worth it if the world comes to know that there is freedom when we serve Christ. Your father and I know this freedom in our hearts even though he is in prison. We found this when we forsook popery and accepted the new faith in Christ. I want to teach you the way of Christ so that you will always be His disciples."

111

The three children gathered around the table on their chairs, and Soetgen got out the copy of the Scriptures she and Willem had used so often.

"My children, it is the will of God that you be just in all your dealings. The Bible teaches that in the way of the just there is life, and in the beaten path there is no death. Again it says, 'It is joy to the righteous to do that which is right, but fear to evildoers.'

"As you get older, choose to earn your bread by the labor of your hands, and to eat your bread with peace. Do not get involved in trading, nor be anxious for great gain. In the Book of Wisdom we read, 'Better is little with the fear of God, than great treasure and trouble therewith. Better is a dry morsel and quietness than a house full of plenty with strife.' "

"Our home is happy," Betken responded, "and we aren't rich."

"That is what I mean," Soetgen answered. "One who is at peace with God and himself doesn't need dainties nor wine. People who desire costly feasts will never be satisfied. You should be content with the labor of your hands. Do not overcharge for your work. Be satisfied with what is reasonable, as you have seen of me. Don't be burdensome to anyone, as long as you can obtain the things needful. Paul says: 'If ye have food and raiment, be therewith content.' "

"Yes," David said, "didn't Paul say, 'It is more blessed to give than to receive'? I hope that I can help others."

"That is the spirit of Christ, David. Follow the examples of the Bible and you will live in the ways

112

of the Lord with sobriety and thankfulness. Let me tell you again of Daniel and his three friends, Shadrach, Meshach, and Abednego. They were selected by the king of Babylon, to be nourished with the same wine and meat which the king drank and ate at his table, in order that they might be beautiful, to serve the king. But they refused his offer and would have nothing but pulse and water! They wanted to observe the law and commandments of their fathers with sobriety and thankfulness in the fear of God. Yet they were fairer and fatter than those who ate of the king's dainties. They were faithful to walk in the ways of God. As they lived by prayer and obedience they made themselves acceptable to God, and He did great things through them. He delivered Daniel from the den of lions, and his three friends out of the fiery furnace."

"Does God always deliver His people like that?" David asked.

"Not always, David, and often when He does, it isn't right away." Soetgen paused, knowing that they were each thinking of their father. Then she continued. "Being delivered from evil in life is even more important than escaping death. A good example of this is Joseph, who was sold by his brothers into Egypt. He avoided dainties, wine, and lust. An Egyptian woman tried to make him do evil, but he feared God, and God preserved him. He pleased God by obedience and prayer, so that in God's time he was appointed ruler over Egypt!"

Soetgen closed the Bible. "Time for bed, my dear ones. Follow these examples in your youth, and you will please God. He will keep you from all evil now, and also when you are older."

During the next few days Soetgen was busier than she had ever been. One Bible study led friends to start another until she was meeting groups all across the region. She couldn't meet with them all, and so she asked others to help. Martha van Leuven was especially capable and soon the two were known as a team, teaching the Word and promoting Christian freedom. Numerous women were converted and began witnessing to their husbands. Some of them responded to the faith of their wives, but several of the men became incensed. They told the bailiff what was happening and urged him to enforce the mandate of the emperor.

Soetgen returned late one evening, to find the door of the house standing open and the children gone. She ran to the barn to see if they were there, but could find no trace of them. Returning to the house she slumped into a chair by the table and buried her face in her hands. "My children, where are they? I've been so busy in the work of God that I've neglected them when they needed me."

Soetgen looked around, but could see nothing in the darkness. "Where are they?"

An old neighbor lady sitting in the darkness answered, "Nettie and Hendrik took them and left. They trusted me. Told me they were going to friends at Oudenaarde tonight, and on to Brugge tomorrow. They can hide out there. Later they may return to your sister Betken."

"At least they're safe," Soetgen breathed. She stood in silence for a moment.

"Where are you going now, Soetgen," the old woman asked.

"I'm not sure where to go." As she thought a moment, the words of Menno Simons crossed her mind, "Always on the run for the sake of the cause, not out of fear, for we live daringly."

The old woman was tugging at her sleeve. "Come, you can stay with me."

"No, I won't endanger you. I have a place to go. I'll go to Martha's. We're in this work together, and I can't harm her. Thank you, Auntie, I must go," and Soetgen embraced her quickly and started along the road.

"God bless you, my dear one," she heard through the darkness, and then she was alone.

The night was dark, but the way was familiar. Only the stars gave her the comfort of light and a sense of direction. She shivered from the cold, drew her shawl more tightly about her and hurried along. At last, nearly at the midnight hour, she stood before Martha's door. She called out as she knocked, hoping her voice would save Martha needless fear.

The door opened quickly. "Soetgen, what brings you here at this hour? Has something happened in Ghent?"

"Not what you think, Martha. I've no word from the prison. But they came for me today while I was gone and took the children."

"To prison?" Martha exclaimed.

"No, they left them with my sister and brother, no doubt expecting to get me later. I learned from old Auntie Frankema that they took them to Oudenaarde and plan to go on to my sister Betken at Brugge. They didn't see me come and go, so I'm here, all alone."

"You must stay here tonight, and we'll think about what to do."

"To do? There isn't much we can do, Martha. They know about our work and mean to stop us. We're both in trouble."

The next morning they discussed their dilemma and prayed together about it. They decided to go to Ghent, believing this would be least expected and that they might be better hid in the crowd. Soetgen wrote a note to the Timmermans, explaining what had happened and urging them to care for the cows and use them as their own. Having sent this by the hand of Martha's neighbor she felt relieved of that concern, and the two started their journey to the city. Both carried a basket and quickly made their way to the familiar site.

At the market they met old friends as usual and sensed that few if any knew they were being sought. They met the Schencks, traders who had moved to Ghent from the Rhine Valley in the East, and arranged for lodging with them.

As they were leaving the market, they met the Kramer family loading their cart to return home. Soetgen and Martha had shared their faith with Mrs. Kramer and she had responded to the gospel and found freedom in Christ. Today her eyes sparkled as she recognized them, but as they approached she quickly looked away. But Mr. Kramer had seen, and a dark scowl crossed his face. Grabbing his wife by the arm, he cried, "Tell me, quick, are these your friends? Are they the ones?"

His wife stood in silence. Soetgen and Martha stopped, stunned by his hostility and suddenly having been made the center of attention of the crowd.

"Heretics," he spat out. Seeing several constables moving through the market, he shouted, "Here, men, quick, here are the heretics you want."

They hurriedly surrounded the women, and before Soetgen and Martha could flee, they were being questioned by one of the constables.

Upon hearing her name, they both cried, "Soetgen van den Houte! We've tramped this country the past two days to find you, and here you are right under our nose. The burgomaster will be mighty pleased about this. You women have become more subtle than the men in the spread of this heresy. Come along, both of you."

Behind them Mr. Kramer was talking excitedly, "Anabaptists, heretics, and I spotted them and turned them in. They won't get away."

As Soetgen turned to look at him, Mrs. Kramer pressed through the circle and caught her hand. "I'm so sorry. He doesn't understand. Please, forgive us."

Soetgen looked into her warm eyes, wet with tears, and smiled wistfully. "Of course, we will, and we'll pray for you. With your new faith you can win him to Christ."

The constables hurried them away, the crowd falling back to make way. Many stood in sullen silence as they went. Soetgen and Martha walked silently between them, prisoners and yet free in their faith.

117

10 The room was small in which Soetgen and Martha were placed. It had only a bench along the wall for their comfort. In the center was a torture block — designed to place a woman on her back, binding her head by tying her hair over the end of the block. A pin stuck out of the wood which would press into the back of her head for increased pain. They each noticed the block, but ignored it as they stumbled to the bench along the wall. Both were exhausted and needed to rest from their long walk. At least they were together for the moment, and not alone.

Shortly after they were imprisoned the bailiff came to their cell door. "Under the mandate of the margrave I will read to you the reason for your arrest."

Unrolling a single brown paper he began to read, "His imperial majesty, King Philip II, commands the Regent Margaret, for the sake of religion and the glory of God, accurately and exactly to cause to be enforced the edicts and decrees made by his imperial majesty Charles V, and renewed by his present majesty, for the extirpation of all sects and heresies."

He rolled the paper in his hand, then said, "You should expect no mercy from us, from the bishop of Arras, nor from the king himself. He has said he would carry the wood to burn his own son were he as wicked as the likes of you."

With this he turned and strode down the hall, leaving the women in stunned silence. After some moments Soetgen spoke slowly and deliberately: "This too will pass. The edict cannot long stand. Those who are for freedom may be forced to stand at bay, but we will not surrender! We are being heard. Though we won't live to see it, this will change. Already the Prince of Orange has heard our witness, and it is known. When King Philip left for Spain he embarrassed the prince publicly by saying that it was he who stood in the way of the Inquisition!"

"I'm sure you are right, Soetgen," Martha replied, "but our lot is clear. We will pay part of the price for religious freedom, and pray that it comes soon."

Through the next week little happened. They only suffered a few jeers from the turnkey as he went about his duties. They tried to get him to tell them of their husbands, but their entreaties fell on deaf ears. At times they heard sounds of torture coming from other chambers. Their food was poor, and their rest was limited. In the middle of the room they could stand upright, but at the edge of the cell they had to crouch because the ceiling was low. They took turns sleeping on the bench. While one slept the other watched to keep off the rats. The stench from corruption on the floor was overpowering, and they took turns breathing fresh air from the narrow opening in the wall. The days were long with no word from outside.

They were finally visited one afternoon by Friar Pieter de Backer, known in Ghent for his subtle betrayal of Anabaptists. He interrogated each in turn, going over simple questions again and again, asking their names, ages, and home backgrounds. He asked when they had embraced this opinion, and how long it had been since they had attended the State Church, and taken the sacrament. He wanted to know of their baptism, who else was present, and who did the baptizing. On the latter questions neither would speak. Finally de Backer turned to Soetgen with a sneer. "You stand alone in your heresy, your family is not with you."

"My husband is with me in the faith."

"Not any longer. Not since the rack and hot lead! We stretched him a foot longer than he was. He was a stubborn one, but he learned."

Soetgen's face turned pale, then flushed, and she stood to her feet, and pointed her finger into his face. "You lie, he has not recanted. I know the depth of his faith."

He backed toward the door. "Little you know in here. You'll hear more of us."

The door closed and Soetgen slumped on the bench. Martha placed an arm over her shoulder. "You must trust, Soetgen. Our men are true, I'm sure."

Soetgen's eyes flashed. "I'm sure, too, but they've nearly killed Wim with torture! We must pray for him." And how they did!

Several days later, de Backer came to their cell again, and repeated his questions, probing for reasons why they had forsaken the obedience and faith of the Holy Church. His interview was brief, and it was soon apparent he had come to deal his major blow in parting. Turning to Soetgen, he said, "Your husband got his today!"

"He what?" she asked.

"The stubborn rascal wouldn't speak, so I couldn't save him."

Her hand flew to her throat. "What happened?"

"They took them out early this morning. He died with four others at the stake. Wouldn't talk before, but stood there and sang while the fire blazed."

Soetgen's face was blanched, and her hands trembled. She sat down on the bench, the hint of a smile played on her face. He sang while the fire blazed! She knew he didn't recant!

De Backer watched her sitting there, then backed out the door. Soetgen sat for some time gazing out the little opening, breathing deeply of the fresh air. Across the city she could see the bell tower, and listened as it pealed out the signals of the evening. The summons for her Willem had come. When would her time be?

The very next morning he was back. He had with him the Dean of Ronse, another inquisitor of repute in Flanders. Immediately they plunged into questioning Soetgen, intent on breaking her.

"Why did you have yourself baptized?"

"The Scripture speaks of a new life. In the New Testament John first called men to repentance, then Christ Himself did so, and afterward the apostles. They taught the people to repent and be baptized. So I repented and was baptized."

He did not say much on this but asked, "Why did you not have your children baptized?"

"I cannot find in the Scriptures that this ought to be done," said Soetgen.

121

"David says: 'I was shapen in iniquity, and in sin did my mother conceive me.' Since children are born with original sin, they must be baptized, if they are to be saved."

"If a man can be saved by an external sign, then Christ has died in vain!" she replied.

"But it is written that we must be born again, of water and of the Spirit; therefore, children must be baptized," he continued.

"Christ does not say this to children, but to the adult. This new birth is God's work, not man's. For this reason I became regenerated. But we know that children are in the hands of the Lord, for the Lord said in Matthew 19:14, 'Suffer little children . . . to come unto me: for of such is the kingdom of heaven.'"

"The household of Stephanas was baptized, according to 1 Corinthians 1:16, which probably also included children," said the inquisitor.

"We do not depend on probabilities; we must have certain assurance."

Again the inquisitor had little to say, then he asked, "What do you think of the Holy Church?"

"I think much of it."

"Why then do you not go to Church?"

"I think nothing of your empty churchgoing."

"Do you believe that God is almighty?"

"Yes, I believe this."

"Do you then also believe that Christ consecrates Himself and is present in the bread? As Paul says in 1 Corinthians 10:16, 'The bread which we break, is it not the communion of the body of Christ? And the cup which we bless, is it not the communion of the blood of Christ?" the inquisitor asked.

"I well know what Paul says, and believe it too," replied Soetgen.

"Christ said in Matthew 26:25, 'Take, eat; this is my body'; and Paul likewise, in 1 Corinthians 11:24."

"I well know what Christ and Paul say, and thus I believe."

"Do you believe that Christ consecrates Himself and is present in the bread?" asked the inquisitor.

"Christ sitteth at the right hand of His Father; He does not come under men's teeth," said Soetgen.

"If you continue in this belief, you will have to go into the abyss of hell forever. It is what all heretics say. Leenaert Bouwens has deceived you; he himself has now renounced his belief, because he saw that he had erred."

"I do not depend on Bouwens or any other man, but only on Christ; He is our foundation, upon whom we have built ourselves, even as Christ teaches us in His gospel: 'Whosoever heareth my words, and doeth them, I will liken him unto a wise man, who built his house upon a rock; and though storms come, and beat against the house, yet it will not fall.' These now are the storms that beat against our house; but Christ is our stronghold, and He will preserve us."

"You do not understand; there are many other writings, of which you know nothing."

"We need no writings other than the holy gospel, which Christ Himself with His blessed lips has spoken to us, and sealed with His blood. If we can observe that, we shall be saved."

"You should suffer yourself to be instructed; the holy

123

fathers instituted church order fifteen hundred years ago!"

"The holy fathers did not have your pattern of holiness; these are human commandments and institutions. Neither did the apostles practice your kind of holiness; I never read it."

"Are you wiser than the Holy Church?" asked the inquisitor.

"I do not wish to do anything against the Holy Church; I have yielded myself to the obedience of the Holy Church, God's true Church," Soetgen replied.

"You should ask yourself: Do I know better than the holy fathers fifteen hundred years ago? You should recognize that you are simple."

"Though I am simple before men, I am not simple in the knowledge of the Lord. Do you not know that the Lord thanked His Father, that He hid these things from the wise and prudent and had revealed them to the simple and unto babes?"

Finally, de Backer looked at the Dean of Ronse, and they nodded to each other, as though the case was hopeless. With their hats in their hands they each turned to the door and left.

Days passed slowly. They were visited by a Jacobine priest who admonished them to repent. He was a large fat man with much talk in him. He tried to get them to name other members of their brotherhood, but to each question they were silent.

"You swear to each other," he cried, "that you will not betray another!"

"We do not swear," Martha replied, "but we do not betray one another."

"Where do you hold your church?"

"Where Christ and His apostles held it," Soetgen answered. "Back of hedges, in the woods, in the fields, on mountains, on the seacoast, sometimes in houses."

"You are tares in the midst of the wheat!"

"If tares, then as Jesus said, let both grow together until the harvest. Why are you a plucker when the plants are not to be plucked up?"

"But your church has no head, or authority, nor do you know one another. You don't even have books in your group older than thirty years."

"The Bible is our book," Soetgen broke in, "from the beginning of the church."

"You talk of faith in Christ, of having your soul saved. What do you know about what your soul is, how large, how long, how wide, or what color it is?"

"What does that concern us?" they replied. "Our salvation does not lie in that! You soul-murderers, you are enemies of the cross of Christ."

He crossed himself over and over and started out of the cell.

"What has your church to offer us?" Martha shouted. "The pope with all his trumpery is good-for-nothing bag and baggage. You priests sell indulgences by the dozens. You preach that one should not drink to excess and you go about the streets drunk as hogs."

He crossed himself again and closed the cell door. As he hurried to the steps, Soetgen called after him, "Bring a Bible next time. We'll show you a better way with the word of the gospel."

The soldiers taunted them daily now with what happened to their husbands. They now administered torture to them in turn on the block. One was forced to watch while the other was being mauled, and then tied to the block for hours. The guards found ways of seeing that both were kept under torture. Soetgen sought to strengthen Martha, but found that in the severity of the treatment each needed to draw special grace from God to bear their lot.

After repeated requests they were given paper on which to write to their friends. This kindness was either to symbolize the finality of their lot, or in the hope they might expose others of their group. Soetgen wrote a lengthy letter to the children, addressing it to a local official who she was sure would deliver it. She knew him to be an accepted representative of the Church and would not be suspect by others in such a deed of kindness.*

Ghent Prison
October 23, 1560

In the name of the Lord:

Grace, peace and mercy from God the Father and the Lord Jesus Christ. This I wish you, my dear little children, David, Betken, and Tanneken, for an affectionate greeting, written by your mother in bonds, for a memorial to you of the truth, as I hope to testify by word and with my death, by the help of the Most High, for an example unto you. May the wisdom of the Holy Ghost instruct and strengthen you therein, that you may be brought up in the ways of the Lord. Amen.

My dear children, since it pleases the Lord to take me

*The full letter which Soetgen wrote is recorded in *Martyrs Mirror* (Scottdale: Mennonite Publishing House, 1968), pp. 646-650.

out of this world, I will leave you a memorial, not of silver or gold; for such jewels are perishable: but I should like to write a jewel into your heart, if it were possible, which is the word of truth, in which I want to instruct you a little for the best with the Word of the Lord, according to the little gift I have received from Him and according to my simplicity.

In the first place, I admonished you, my most beloved, always to suffer yourself to be instructed by those who fear the Lord; then you will please God, and as long as you obey good admonition and instruction, and fear the Lord, He will be your Father and not leave you orphans. For David says: "What man is he that feareth the Lord? him shall he teach in the way that he shall choose." Ps. 25:12. He also says: "The eye of the Lord is upon them that fear him, upon them that hope in his mercy; to deliver their soul from death. The angel of the Lord encampeth round about them that fear him; O fear the Lord, ye his saints, for there is no want to them that fear him; for the fear of the Lord is the beginning of wisdom. Ps. 33:18, 19; 34:7, 9; 111:10.

David, my dear child, I herewith commend you to the Lord. You are the oldest, learn wisdom, that you may set your sisters a good example; and beware of bad company, and of playing in the street with bad boys; but diligently learn to read and write, so that you may get understanding. Love one another, without contention or quarreling; but be kind to each other.

Love your enemies, and pray for those who speak evil of you, and afflict you. Rather suffer wrong, than that you should grieve another; rather suffer affliction, than that you should afflict another; rather be reproached, than that you should reproach another; rather be slandered, than that you should slander another; rather be robbed, than that you should rob another; rather be beaten, than that you should beat another, and so forth.

Further, my dear children, Betken and Tanneken, my

127

beloved lambs, I admonish you in all these same things, as that you obey the commandments of the Lord, and also obey your uncle and aunt and your elders, and all who instruct you in virtue.

See, my most beloved, when you have attained the years of understanding, see that you adorn yourselves with good works, namely, the works of the Spirit, that is, with all manner of goodness, gentleness, meekness, humility, obedience, long-suffering, righteousness, modesty, honorableness, purity, peaceableness, steadfastness, mercifulness, wisdom, diligence in good works, faith, hope, and love; to love God above all that is in the world, and to do to your neighbor as you would have men do unto you, on which hang all the law and the prophets. Gal. 5:22, 23; Matt. 22:37, 40.

My dear children, this I leave you as a memorial or testament. If you put it to good use, you will gather more treasure by it, than if I had left you many riches, which are perishable; for the riches of this world may be lost through fire, war, or misfortune.

Therefore covet no one's property or treasures; nor envy any one because he has more than you. Neither regard any person for his gifts, but follow the little flock, who walk truly in love; for love is the bond of perfectness, and the command of love is superior to all others. Luke 12:32; Col. 3:14. Therefore, see constantly that you follow those who walk in love before all men; for Christ was hated too, and the servant is not better than his lord. Matt. 10:24.

Herewith I will bid you adieu: adieu my dear children, and adieu all my friends.

My most beloved, though our adversaries tell you, that your father and I are not of the same faith, do not believe them; for he confessed the truth concerning baptism and the incarnation of Christ, in all that he was able to comprehend, and he valiantly testified to righteousness, giving his life for it, pointing out to you for an example, the

128

same way which the prophets, the apostles and Christ Himself went. He had to go before through the conflict with much tribulation and suffering, and leave his children behind for Christ's sake; hence do likewise, for there is no other way. Give diligence to read the Testament. Amen.

Your Mother, Soetgen van den Houte

The letter mailed, Soetgen somehow felt better about the children. She would leave them in God's care. No matter what they heard of Willem's death, they would know that she was certain he had stood with her in faith.

She and Martha both noted a difference in the Inquisition during the next several weeks. The questions now pertained more to death and being prepared for their martyrdom. Together they pondered the mystery of death and the assurance they had of a greater life beyond this one. They discussed this together and prayed much, conditioning their own minds for the inevitable. There were times that the presence of God was so real in their cell that its drab and sinister walls seemed transformed into a hallowed sanctuary.

Nearly a week later the guard came to their cell with a letter for Soetgen. Her heart quickened as he handed it to her, but he held on to it. "You should be grateful that we are delivering this letter; we needn't, you know."

"I know," Soetgen replied calmly, "but what would you do with a farewell note? Your heart is hard enough not to be moved by it."

"Take it," he hissed. "There won't be any more."

Soetgen sat down on the little bench by the opening

where she could see. Her hands trembled as she
unrolled the scroll. A small paper enclosed in the roll
fluttered to the floor. As she picked it up, her heart
surged as she recognized the familiar writing of little
Betken. The tears ran down her face and splashed
on the paper as she read:

To our dearest mother:
   We miss you so very much, and pray for you every
day. Tanneken and David are well, and both are telling
me what to write. Tanneken says not to worry about us,
that we are being good, that we hope those mean men
will soon let you come home. David says to tell you he
promises to look out for us, and that we will be faithful
disciples of Christ.
   Uncle and Aunt send you their greetings. They help us
in our studies and in our reading of the Scriptures. Aunt
Nettie is helping me write this letter. David and Tanneken
are going to Aunt Betken's for a short stay, as she wants
David to help with some work.
   I can only say that we miss you very much, that we
remember your teaching, and that I will always try to
be a woman like you.
   We have read your letter many times, and promise
that we will live by your teachings, as you have taught
us of Christ. We will seek to live by His commandment
of love, and by His Spirit, and be honest in life and
true in faith.
   Good-bye for now. Each of us send our love.
                              Your daughter, Betken.

Soetgen sat in silence for a while. The tears were
dry now; her grief was beyond that stage. Martha
watched her without speaking — her lips moved only
in prayer. She turned next to the letter from Nettie
and Hendrik. A smile crossed her face as she read

Nettie's words about the children, about their under-standing and faith, and the promise to look after the children if she should be sacrificed. Her heart surged with joy at Nettie's own words of comfort, for in them there was evidence of her own personal faith. Soetgen was sure now that Nettie too followed Christ.

She handed the letters to Martha and gave her the bench. "Read them. You'll enjoy their faith too."

And for the next several days those pages were read again and again, until blurred from use and tears. They had read into every sentence all they could, both from interpretation and from their memories.

"The world will change, Martha. This will pass. My daughters will live as free women, and my son as a man of God among men. I know it."

"Yes," Martha whispered, "that is our hope, and hope is never embarrassed."

A few mornings later the guard rapped sharply on the cell door and handed them each a roll of parchment. His manner was exceedingly brisk. "This is for your last will and testament. You have only a short time to write it before the stake. Get to it if you want to leave anything at all."

They looked at each other in silence a moment, as the sound of his steps receded in the corridor. Then a fleeting smile crossed Martha's face — "Leave any-thing? We're leaving, but only before the harvest. 'Except a corn of wheat fall into the ground and die, it abideth alone.'"

"Yes," Soetgen responded. "This is our hour; this is the moment we've expected. Now let's trust the Holy Spirit to strengthen us to die nobly."

131

Martha shivered from the intense cold. "At least some warmth will be a change from being half-frozen."

Soetgen looked at Martha's wry smile and added, "It won't last long, Martha, and it will all be over — we'll soon be free. Thank God that women can leave a witness of joy and freedom."

Each sat on the bench alone with her thoughts. Soetgen began to write, addressing her letter to Nettie and Hendrik, who now shared her faith. She was sure they would share it with the children, and she would ask them to pass it on to her sister Betken.

Ghent Prison
Nov. 27, 1560

Written out of love:

The peace of the Lord be with you; my dear brother and sister, know that I have received two letters, with their contents, and I thank you most cordially for all the friendship you have ever shown me, and shall yet show me, I hope, in my three lambs whom I leave behind, commending them to the Lord and to those whom He shall direct thereto in His grace.

Herewith I take leave once more; I think it is now the last time. We are of such good cheer to offer up our sacrifice that I cannot express it. I could leap for joy when I think of the eternal riches which are promised to us as our inheritance, and to all who persevere in what the Lord has commanded us. Matt. 10:22.

I know not how I shall praise the Lord that He has chosen Martha and myself to this estate, us who are such poor, simple lambs, for we have never been esteemed in the world, except as outcasts; and that God has chosen such rejected, miserable, simple worms of the dust, that He will work through us, that we should be His witnesses, we who are not worthy of ourselves to receive the very least gift which the Lord might bestow, etc.

Oh, who can comprehend the power of God, that He should be most merciful to those who are here the most rejected, if they call upon Him with confidence and firmly place their hope in His grace unto the end; it were impossible that the Lord should reject them. Hence I pray all that love the Lord, that they humble their hearts, for the Lord says through the prophet Isaiah "I will dwell with him that is of a contrite Spirit, and of a broken heart, and trembleth at my word." Isa. 57; 66:2.

Yea, those who thus humble themselves before the Lord, and do not think themselves to be something before God, and before men, them shall God exalt and enrich with heavenly riches. Matt. 23:12. Remember how Christ chose humility, when He left the glory of His Father and descended into the lower parts of the earth. From obedience to His Father, and out of great love He became man; with great humility He came to serve us, suffered pain and reproach, enduring it with patience and long-suffering, out of obedience to His Father, even unto death, until He had finished all, so that He might save us. Phil. 2:8. Oh, what love did He show us by His anxiety and sighing, when He said according to His humanity: "How am I straitened till it be accomplished!" Luke 12:50.

O my most beloved, consider our Leader, Jesus Christ, how He regarded the humility of Mary that He would be born of her. And though she was chosen to such a high estate, she humbled herself, saying: "Behold the handmaid of the Lord. For God hath regarded the low estate of his handmaiden; therefore, henceforth all generations shall call me blessed. For his mercy is on them that fear him from generation to generation; for he hath scattered the proud. He hath put down the mighty from their seats, and exalted them of low degree. He hath filled the hungry with good things, and the rich hath he sent empty away. To the poor the gospel is preached. Blessed are they which do hunger and thirst after righteousness; for they shall be filled." Luke 1:38, 48; etc.; 7:22; Matt. 5:6.

O my dearest, my heartfelt desire and request is, for the last time, that you give diligence to walk in love, simplicity, and harmony among yourselves, always in the fear of God, that you may be filled with the heavenly good things, and satisfied now and forever. Amen.

Herewith I commend you to the Lord, and to the Word of His grace. May He comfort, strengthen, stablish you all with His Spirit, that you may finish that whereunto you are called, to the praise and glory of the Lord, so that you may rejoice together, and sit down at the Lord's table, where He shall serve us with new wine, in the kingdom of God, His Father.

This was written when we had eaten our last supper, as far as we know. Herewith I bid adieu to all my brethren and sisters. I and Martha, my sister in the Lord, salute you much with the peace of the Lord, for the last time all who are known to us or not, wherever they be. We rejoice in the Lord, we bid adieu till we meet above, in the New Jerusalem. Heb. 12:22.

Read this last farewell to all who desire to hear it, before you send it away; and then send it to my sister Betken.

Further, my dear child Betken, I rejoice greatly that the Lord spared me so long, that I was made glad before my death through your letter, by which you have strengthened me. I pray the Lord to strengthen and confirm you with His Spirit, that you may go on thus, and follow that which is best, as you wrote to me.

O my dear lambs, see that you do not spend your youth in vanity, or pride, or drinking, or gluttony, but in sobriety and humility in the fear of God, clothed with the adornment of the saints, so that God may make you worthy through His grace, to enter into the marriage of the Lamb, and that we may see you there with joy. Your father and I, and many others, have shown you the way. Take an example from the prophets and apostles, yea, Christ Himself, who all went this way; and where the Head has gone before, there the members must certainly follow.

Herewith I will commend you to the Lord, and to the Word of His grace. This is my last farewell, my dear lambs; always remember each other in love; learn the better to read and write, and obey everyone in that which is good. When your brother David and Tanneken come to you, greet one another with a friendly kiss of peace, in my name.

Herewith I bid you adieu, my dear child, Betken; adieu, my dear children David and Tanneken; adieu, all my dear brethren and sisters, and friends everywhere.

Once more we say adieu; greet uncle and aunt much with the kiss of peace, in my name.

Written by me Soetgen van den Houte, your mother in bonds; written in haste (while trembling with cold), out of love for you all. Amen.°

She sat in silent prayer over her letter — her last words to her family. The sound of voices and of steps on the stairs announced the coming of the guard. She could hear them now, coming down the hall toward their cell. Quickly she wrote at the end:

This is my moment to meet our Lord with joy. The cup He permits, I will drink. Farewell, they have come for me.

°From *Martyrs Mirror*, pp. 650, 651.

The Author

Myron S. Augsburger was born at Elida, Ohio. He received the AB and ThB degrees from Eastern Mennonite College, Harrisonburg, Va., the BD degree from Goshen College Biblical Seminary, Goshen, Ind., and the ThD degree from Union Theological Seminary, Richmond, Va.

He was ordained to the ministry in 1951 as pastor of the Tuttle Avenue Mennonite Church, Sarasota, Fla. For four years he was pastor of students at Eastern Mennonite College, Harrisonburg, Va. In July, 1965, he became president of Eastern Mennonite College.

He had served with great effectiveness as an evangelist, both in congregational meetings and in community crusades which are sponsored by Inter-Church Evangelism, Inc., Atglen, Pa. This ministry has taken him into many parts of the United States and Canada, as well as to Jamaica, India, and the Near East. His community crusades are conducted in city auditoriums. As evangelist with Inter-Church Evangelism, he has engaged in this evangelistic program for the past fifteen years.

He is author of *Called to Maturity* (1960), *Quench Not the Spirit* (1962), *Invitation to Discipleship* (1964), *Principles of Biblical Interpretation* (1966), *Pilgrim Aflame* (1967).

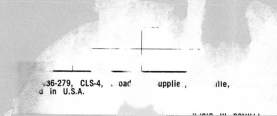

36-279, CLS-4, oad upplie, ile,
d in U.S.A.

The castle-prison at Ghent

The castle at Antwerp